GAMES BEYOND FRONTIERS

A Football Fan's Odyssey

Richard Brentnall

Published by Sigma Leisure – an imprint of
Sigma Press, 1 South Oak Lane, Wilmslow, Cheshire SK9 6AR, England.

British Library Cataloguing in Publication Data
A CIP record for this book is available from the British Library.

ISBN: 1-85058-739-6

Typesetting and Design by: Sigma Press, Wilmslow, Cheshire.

Printed by: MFP Design & Print

Cover Design: The Agency, Macclesfield

Introduction

I used to be herded like a cow at railway stations and escorted like a convict through city streets. I was a mindless pariah, and because I couldn't be trusted I almost became tagged and regulated by a special identity card. In the words of one former Minister for Sport I possessed an "effluent tendency", and this island should have been my prison. There was nobody like me in an otherwise responsible society, and I was peculiar to this country.

Nowadays, I am viewed rather differently. I am not merely tolerated. Celebrities and politicians profess interest in my world, because they now see my world as being in vogue, and the latter wish me to look kindly upon them and give them my vote. A television company has based its expansion strategy upon coverage of my world and thereby my money.

I have always loved my world. I am capable of rational thought and morality. I have pursued my love beyond the frontiers of national borders and of people's perception of me.

I was, and am, an English football fan. Here are some of my experiences over the years.

Richard Brentnall

Dedication

To Frank, who forewent his golf for my football; and to Patricia, forever inspirational despite God's mysterious intervention.

Contents

Chapter 1
Ossie Induces a Sea-Change

Argentina: Huracán v Estudiantes 12/6/93

The dingy sidestreet is deserted and mostly in darkness, and I am irrigating it. This early Sunday hour isn't silent, though, because the chilly waterfront air is being pierced by a bar that's still in full swing a few yards from where I lurch. Through its hubbub rise the melancholy strains of tango. The sidestreet is in La Boca. Amid my fascination at the rivulet's choice of meander into its gutter I am praying for a taxi, and now I glimpse the light of a vehicle approaching slowly. I hope he'll stop despite the state I'm in, and hearing a door slam I turn my head to greet him. But there's no cabbie. Instead, there are two men standing behind me, uniformed and with truncheons drawn. I roll my eyes and then, in body language that pathetically pleads an innocence of sorts, I hunch my shoulders and have my left arm fashion some apologetic gesture. My right hand, meanwhile, assumes a more protective grip of the rivulet's still active source. Eventually, the uniforms unimpressed, their truncheons motion me to join their car. Its back seat.

Through my sudden pronounced unease, I am nevertheless struck by the sheer size of the wagon. There is room for three others in the back: though I am sandwiched by only two. But there is also room, curiously, for three in the front: though again there are only two. So. I am in the custody of just the four police officers as they maintain cruising speed through the shadowy backstreets of Buenos Aires.

I snatch a look at the one on my right. In his late forties, he is an identikit not only of some beefy, swarthy South American señor but also, alarmingly to the imagination, of someone who once might routinely have emptied military aircraft of political dissidents into the South Atlantic. I thank time's march that there is no longer any Dirty War from which I too might disappear. But then I think of another war, the one waged by Galtieri and Thatcher for brownie points at the expense of young men's lives, and hope urgently that there are no serious grudges – Lord forbid out of bereavement – enveloping someone who has just pissed on their territory.

I don't speak much Spanish. And despite my reawakening I slur anyway. "Look. I am very sorry. I had no choice."

I look again at Pancho Machismo. There is no movement around his fungus moustache and like the others, deadpan, he looks at the road ahead which continues to slide slowly beneath us. The silence continues for several minutes, or perhaps hours.

"You have money?"

Oh right. So this is where they're coming from. I have everything, and I mean everything, in a pouch strapped to my left shin. "No, it's in my hotel."

I now wonder all the more where they're going to.

"Which your hotel?"

I see little point in telling cute lies on this score. Except that I now realise I can't remember its name anyway. I know where it is right enough, but that's all.

"Avenida de Mayo."

More silence. Eventually the streets become wider with more lights and more people, but I don't recognise any of it. I am still utterly cold-shouldered and assume I could have saved forking out for my digs. Truncheons still cross laps. Will the cells be padded, I wonder. I now attempt nervously to rise above the heightening dread in my stomach by drawing upon something whose popularity is so global that it may even extend to these sullen, corrupt ogres. "You like futbol?"

I look to the one on my left, who might be the one on my right's younger brother. He glances at me, then away again. The shotgun, though, turns around and stares at me. I proceed to rattle off the names of all the heroes I can think of, given my circumstances.

"Ardiles, Passarella, Kempes...." I spit the next name from my mind's list and hope no facial expression betrays such contempt. "....Maradona...."

Shotgun turns back and mutters to the driver. They chuckle: which is something. I steal another glance at Pancho and detect a faint smile, which heartens me just a little.

The city centre is upon us, and busy. Strangely, the wagon halts. I peer out of its windows but see no police station. Pancho, however, climbs out and leaves his door open. He beckons me out, then sweeps a geographical arm. "Avenida de Mayo. Go to hotel. And do not go again where you go tonight."

Studying me, he shakes his head and makes a cut-throat sign. I breathe deeply upon my relief. I am so relieved that I offer him my hand. He shakes that, too. And then they are gone. A few minutes later, sitting by my hotel window, I draw on a fag and think over my first twenty hours in this place.

It was June 1993 and at last I'd got round to fulfilling this particular ambition: to visit – at least part of it – South America. In my infant football mind, names such as Pelé, Didi, Sivori and di Stefano had held magic. In my later school-days, words such as Andes, Mato Grosso, Incas, Pampas and conquistadores were ones to conjure wildly with. This fascination with the continent's geography, history and football would be fuelled fondly each time panpipes or tango entered my living room. Smugly unappreciative remarks, however, have occasionally been aired in that room upon discovery of my Edmundo Ros collection.

And there were those among my acquaintances who'd looked upon my choice of holiday destination with surprise bordering on sniffy disapproval. For Argentina was a land of bastards, especially when it came to playing England in World Cups, not to mention when it came to sneaky manoeuvres. Upon my return home, I would receive smirking looks that said, "What did I tell you?" – but more later of the cause of those.

For fans of England's national team, two countries above all induce hatred, Germany of course being the other. This is because we have fallen foul of this pair in crucial matches; and there is also the inescapable link between such loathing and the more pressing matter of twentieth-century warfare. But whilst the Germans have demanded a parallel grudging respect because of their perennial competitiveness, never-say-die spirit and, damn it, sheer success, the Argentinians have earned nothing of the sort. They have been seen as greasy, violent and without scruple. England has fallen foul of them in more ways than one.

The first disservice they did me was in my own back garden. The afternoon of July 19th 1966 was a gloriously sunny one as it drew towards the hour when I needed to catch a bus into Nottingham from where my dad had organised a lift to Hillsborough. To get into the mood for this World Cup Group 2 match I was indulging in a spot of keepy-uppy and to my astonishment I absolutely demolished my record as my feet refused to err, my body finding a rhythm as unearthly as that heavenly one it would find in later years in another kind of activity. The third time my mother shouted my name from the kitchen window I had no choice but to abort this unreal episode and volley my plaything hard against the shed in aggrieved unfulfilment. I was precisely one hundred and twenty-seven short of a thousand. I had to go and watch Argentina play Switzerland.

Four days later the first real seeds of detestation were sown. I still possess my ticket for the West Germany v Uruguay quarter-final at Sheffield, unused because how on earth could anyone possibly miss the televised game at Wembley? This match was seminal on two counts: in the shorter term, it was one where England's victory ignited real hopes that an ultimate triumph was something not beyond us; in the longer term, it implanted in the minds of Englishmen a contempt for Argentina which still burns today with or without the paraffin of subsequent events. The irony of this Saturday afternoon, though, was that even Argentina's ten men, after Rattin's sending off, still looked so accomplished that had the side concentrated from the start on playing within the rules they might in that way have pulled off a result. Instead, the ten maintained the despicable emphasis of the eleven upon spoiling – to put it mildly – and vilification was let loose for life. Ramsey's famous condemnation remains unforgiven in Buenos Aires and beyond to this day, or to my knowledge anyway until June 1993 at least. What many people won't be aware of is that Argentina's players compounded their misdeeds upon the Wembley pitch by urinating in its corridors, although vengeful remembrance of this fact was absent as I teetered in La Boca.

Dreamily, two and a half years after England's conquest, I had found myself sharing the employer of the English Knight hated upon that continent which held so much allure for me. The FA was without a commissionaire in my earliest days at Lancaster Gate, and so it was that midway through each afternoon I would be required to leave my junior's desk to man the reception. I was still short of my eighteenth birthday, disorientated, rather friendless, and prone to homesickness. The only person who stopped on numerous occasions to spend time with me, on his way home to Ipswich, was none other. It is impossible, of course, to ever forget Sir Alf Ramsey, but nor will I forget the fact that he, unlike others, could indeed be arsed to have a word. During my exploration of Argentina I would find myself in a hotel bar in Colón, watching the national side play Bolivia in the South American Championships, in the company of a person who spoke fair English. He slagged off Sir Alf. I responded.

After 1966, twenty years would elapse before England and Argentina crossed swords again in the World Cup. Those years would not be without that paraffin.

"They played rough, and we chickened out." How ironic indeed that an Argentinian should have so bemoaned. "Only four of us had any guts." These words were spoken by Pancho Varallo in recalling the first World Cup Final of 1930, lost to their rivals across the murky River Plate in Montevideo. Forty years on, and the reputation of Argentinian club sides had become so odious that teams simply refused to play them. The nadir of their moral corruption was reached in the so-called World Club Championship of 1970. British fans had already been outraged by the excesses of Racing against Celtic and Estudiantes against Manchester United, where cynicism and violence had consigned football to insignificance. But the depths of nastiness were plumbed when Joop van Daele's reward for scoring Feyenoord's winner was to have his spectacles promptly smashed by Estudiantes' Pachame. Ajax's leads in declining to participate the following year against Nacional of Uruguay and against Argentina's Independiente in 1973 would be followed by the likes of Bayern Munich and Liverpool, who considered sharing a pitch with Independiente and Boca Juniors not worth the risk to valuable limbs. It would eventually be left to, er, Toyota to restore some respectability to a contest which had been so soured by the clash between psyches of Latin America and northern Europe.

For Argentina itself to incur disdain in the late seventies and early eighties is easily assimilated, but quite how its football should degenerate to the point where it became viewed with repugnance – an emotion frequently invited for a quarter of a century and more from the mid-sixties onwards – is a matter more complex. Drag along with you a psyche, which involves perhaps an overly patriotic streak born of a relatively new and turbulent nation and also the prickly element of Latin machismo, as you pursue a new direction that is perhaps overly pragmatic; add a siege mentality and a stubborn refusal to acquiesce that develop in proportion to the insults tossed your way over the years; and there you may have part of the cause.

The pragmatic new direction had its root in Argentina's lamentable reappearance upon the World Cup stage in 1958, their first participation in the finals for twenty-four years. Such was their failure – including a 1–6 annihilation by Czechoslovakia – that when they arrived home, their aeroplane taxied into a hangar to escape the wrath of waiting fans. A revision of approach was deemed to be required: an erstwhile reliance upon mere technical merit was impotent in the face of teams who were fitter and paid more tactical attention to the threat posed by opponents. This new, unromantic attitude quickly revealed itself in Argentina's domestic football, now being ever more denuded of its better performers who chased fame and fortune in Europe. By the mid-sixties the world game would see players deployed more prudently still and a greater use of physicality; success on the international stage demanded that these elements be combated. Whilst the Brazilians would find it quite alien to their instinct in misguidedly attempting to follow such a course in 1974 (probably the worst Brazil team ever to participate in the World Cup Finals, and which paled in comparison with Holland: football had by then moved on further), Argentinians were more disposed to trench warfare as the sixties unfolded. To win at any cost thus came to characterise their game. If the high priest of catenaccio was Inter Milan's Helenio Herrera, a son of Buenos Aires, then leading Machiavellian lights closer to home were Juan Carlos

Lorenzo, responsible for the 1966 World Cup team, and Osvaldo Zubeldia, his predecessor, who would then turn Estudiantes into a synonym for depravity.

By 1986 Argentina had succeeded in lifting the World Cup twice, but when the final whistle sounded in Mexico City, for all that it had been the Germans whom they'd beaten 3–2, their stock in the eyes of Englishmen had probably never been lower. The war in the South Atlantic was still large in our consciousness, and our nation's football fans now had another act to grind their teeth upon. A dispassionate consideration of the incident would lay blame squarely with the match officials for an incredible failure of any of them to notice; but World Cup quarter-finals are anything but passionless and Maradona was, simply, a cheating little clitoris, and blasphemous with it, never to be forgiven. If his marvellous second goal served to crystallise the acceptable component of not only his own but Argentina's historically flawed genius, then that other one crystallised our hatred of his country. Four years later we would view their craven passage in defence of their title with more contempt and welcome their defeat in another final, even though their attempt perished at the hands of West Germany, who indulged in skulduggery of their own. And a year after that we would be infuriated once again by their antics at Wembley when, with the evident approval of their new manager Basile, he of that infamous Racing team of 1967, Argentinian shirts would be twirled overhead in leaving the pitch with the same naked provocation that had seen Nigel Clough's face visited by Fernando Gamboa's spittle: "a great big gozza – a green phlegmy one," as described graphically by Graham Taylor.

Within hours of landing at Ezeiza airport, and prior to my evidently risky sampling of La Boca's cantinas, I squatted high on the terracing at the Estadio Tomas Aldolfo Duco, home of Huracán, one of more than twenty professional clubs in the sprawling metropolis of Buenos Aires.

Founded in 1908, Huracán had won four league championships in the 1920s but since the advent of professionalism in 1931, although still bracketed as one of the 'big six' clubs in Argentina, had added just one more. That was in 1973, and its significance lay in the name of the manager who delivered it to them. The architect of Argentina's first World Cup success in 1978 was a man who remarkably, in aiming for this pinnacle of achievement, had determined that it would be sought in a fashion which had been long since forsaken. There would be a retrieval of positivity to replace negativity; intent would be rooted not in cynicism but in fairness of spirit; the team would, for as long as it was in his charge, have a heart beating to play pure football. This man would never betray his ideals. He was Cesar Luis Menotti, and Huracán had been his stage before the national flag fluttered to his door. I wanted to pay his old stage a visit. But there was more.

As my eyes trailed around the stadium they imagined someone else from yesteryear, a little pixie who'd left the provincial city of Córdoba to make his name here too. Whilst that name will always be synonymous with another English club, it had just given the kiss-of-life to my own, which I'd supported since the age of seven despite my Nottingham childhood. Two years earlier the shirt once worn by Pennington and Richardson, Allen and Barlow, Cunningham and the Robsons, had been consigned unthinkably to the old third division and West Bromwich Albion, in its shame and impotence, was being sucked towards oblivion. Then a new manager arrived, implanted a new heart beating to play pure football never mind the pub league it was in, in a style that recalled our best tradition, and had just got us promoted in his first season. To him, I shall be eternally grateful. I loved Ossie Ardiles. I loved an Argentinian. If ever I'd met him I might have found it irresistible to cuddle him. As someone who once ended an evening's drinking session up in Kirkcaldy with Willie Johnston by planting a kiss on that little firebrand's forehead, this would not have been surprising.

Huracán's ground, on this day, exuded a ghostliness in more ways than one. Its current capacity was 48,000 and once upon a golden age it might have reverberated to drums beating and hordes boinging (in best Baggies style) as opponents of the calibre of Pedernera, Labruna or di Stefano strutted their romantic stuff – the latter actually spent a year on loan to Huracán in the mid-forties. Now, though, its large uncovered bowl was virtually deserted for this meaningless last home match of the season. A sizeable mob, true, sang encouragement from my near right to be met by whistles from the thirty-odd visitors dotting the opposite end, but most of the remaining space was just that, revealing sadly how neglected the place had become. It certainly wouldn't have earned a safety certificate in England: the eroded terracing where I camped – steep, ridged and bewilderingly irregular concrete steps parlously short of crush barriers – must surely have threatened danger for any healthy gathering, especially given the wont of Latin football supporters to surge forward in celebration. A quarter of a century earlier, this had indeed been a scene of death, though that had nothing to do with decomposing architecture. A fifteen-year-old visitor had been slaughtered by Huracán fans minutes before a match against Racing in April 1967, Argentina's first terrace fatality caused by spectator confrontation (many more would follow) as opposed to police brutality.

The pitch, too, was a mess, uneven with grass too long. Unsurprisingly it was populated by players whose names were unfamiliar to me, with one glaring exception. At centre-back for Huracán was Pedro Monzón who in 1990, when with Independiente, had become the first man to be sent off in a World Cup Final. The players of both sides here were positive enough and it was good to see the game played mostly on the floor, though it was riddled with error as much as it was graced by clever touch. I noticed no budding new Ossies or Housemans, Brindisis or Babingtons. The most accomplished looking performer on view was the balding Dalla Líbera, Huracán's midfield playmaker, and it was he who scored the clincher a minute before half-time, Huracán recovering from conceding an early goal to win 2–1. Remarkably, there were no sendings-off; the visiting team, like Huracán safe in mid-table, had managed to accumulate an astonishing thirteen red cards in their eighteen matches prior to this afternoon, and even more mind-blowingly had seen eighteen opponents dismissed too. Huracán's opposition was Estudiantes. Little surprise there, then.

As the stadium emptied into the swallowing suburban streets, like an almost dead pint glass being finished off, I trod a careful course to its bottom. Standing by Menotti's old bench I gazed around for the last time, amazed at how tall, almost suffocating, the grey old stands looked as they pressed tightly towards the pitch where Ossie had learned his trade, flitting through tackles, fashioning his one-twos, spearing home his goals, playing Menotti's brand of inventive, lyrical football in a way he would later wish for my own team as he steered it, hopefully, towards a return to the top flight. In the bar next door I mentioned their names. I drew wistful smiles.

So, on my second day here and with a fortnight at my disposal, I would begin a wider tour of this infamous land: one that, fascinated or not, a part of me had reviled spanning three decades and more because of its football teams. I'd discover its geography, training my eye upon its reality whilst recalling wistfully my exercise books of yesterschoolyear; and I'd discover its people, wondering how many might be as lovable as Ardiles, as surprisingly considerate as Pancho Machismo, as spirited as those I'd seen partying in La Boca, or as sheer nasty as Fernando Gamboa. The second discovery would indeed be revealing.

I received my first inkling on my second night, still in Buenos Aires. The differences from the previous night were that I was sober, and therefore cognisant, and I was in the teeming central area of the Avenidas Santa Fe and Corrientes. Two days earlier Eduardo de Simone, one of its officials, had announced that the government was to pursue an investigation into British shootings of Argentine prisoners during the Falklands War. "Veterans will be able to make their comments heard anywhere in the country," he stated. I remembered this as I sat, feeling somewhat like the proverbial spare prick at the wedding, and was now required to give the waiter my order, audibly to those who surrounded me. I became not the unwanted intruder but remained the spare prick, and the meal was uninterruptedly delicious.

There was something of Huracán in Buenos Aires itself. You could sense a golden olden age, but also be aware of a Madrid-like elegance somewhat faded. Yet, contrarily, there was nothing of Huracán today in the city's nevertheless rich liveliness, where people – ordinary folk, and bustling to do so – dine well past midnight even when there's work to be done the same day. I found Buenos Aires' heartbeat to be terrific before leaving it, for a while, the next day.

This day, like Sunday, was saturating. It was all the more wet because nowhere, including the tourist office I was seeking, was open. I just couldn't weigh it up until I wandered upon a café doing business next to a taxi rank. I was then handed not only a brandy but also the smiling everyday information that today was Malvinas Day. So much for that, then. Taxi drivers in Buenos Aires, truncheon carrying or not, are usually honest, and this one now took me to the ferry port without overcharge and without rancour either. Christ, he even patted my shoulder as I got out despite his tip being merely the tiny change.

Uruguay, filthy bastards in the 1986 World Cup but never to the detriment of England, was my mysterious port of call before rejoining Argentina. The rejoining would be somewhat awkward after three days' touring during which I'd sat in a deserted Estadio Centenario, the scene that had so begot Pancho Varallo's disgust. Whilst in the bantering company of a Nacional-supporting owner and a Peñarol-supporting drinker in a backstreet Paysandú bar, I'd contrived to miss the last bus across the border, and the taxi which subsequently carried me out of Uruguay over the Artigas Bridge towards Colón was required to stand at the checkpoint for several minutes as I underwent a searching interview; I'd consigned to an Ezeiza bin a visitor's document that was now vital as opposed to inconsequential. Thankfully the office uniforms charitably allowed for the innocence of a traveller far from home.

My far from innocent prejudice towards certain things Argentine was now, following on from my admiration for downtown Buenos Aires, about to be dealt a lesson. I was to find a country and its people that would shame any myopic preconceptions. Gringos are despised because the Malvinas belong to Argentina and poor boys were slaughtered by ruthless pirates. Well, the British aren't so despised. Galtieri's opportunist invasion was a last throw of the dice by the military dictatorship and its abject failure precipitated a new government by democracy for its terribly repressed people. The seven-year Dirty

War, the omnipresent terror of the Generals, were thus no more. This is why I met no antagonism. This is indeed how I experienced acceptance, nay, friendliness, a politeness sometimes bordering surprisingly upon meekness. I felt pleased for the people, and even slightly sorry that their souvenirs would show Passarella being handed their World Cup by such a monster as Jorge Videla.

I took a coach to Puerto Iguazú in the province of Misiones, by Argentina's far north-eastern borders with Brazil and Paraguay, the area featured in the celebrated film that saw De Niro and Irons portraying the eighteenth-century struggles of the Jesuits. Of all Argentina's diverse wonders, whether beholding the magnificent Andes or perhaps the glacial wilderness of southern Patagonia, there surely cannot be a sight to compare with here, perhaps not in the whole of South America. Those who consider themselves to be special on God's earth should stand on a catwalk bestriding the Iguazú Falls, five times the size of Niagara. A more humbling experience is barely imaginable. As the waters rumbled, roared and crashed and spray lashed miniature rainbows, I'd never felt so insignificant as I did now amid such raw, natural majesty, deafening and intoxicating, violent in the mist. Nor will I forget the lusciousness of the jungle's fiery sunset as I left.

I'd thought it not a bad idea to send Ossie a postcard from his homeland: after all, I now felt I loved both.

But that course, as they say, never runs smooth .....

The Iguazú Falls

My eighteen-hour journey back to Buenos Aires still had 300 kilometres to do, and at eight-thirty in the morning most of the coach was still asleep. I'd just polished off the breakfast served by the attractive blonde courier who'd been giving me the eye and, in true romantic fashion, had put on a Spandau Ballet tape. I was at peace with the world. Moments later I spotted that the relief driver seated not far away had turned to the football pages of his newspaper, and I duly leaned forward to try and catch any snippets about the Copa América (which Argentina would win), wondering which match I might be watching in some bar later on. My eye hadn't trailed far when the thunderbolt struck. The first thing in the photograph I noticed was Ossie. The other two things were Alan Sugar and a Tottenham shirt, which they were holding up between them as they shook hands. Although roughly one third of his size, Ossie had done a Big Ron and a runner from Halfords Lane.

Only one word left my lips but its delivery carried such decibels that the entire coach was now rudely awake. While Tony Hadley warbled out 'Only When You Leave' with unknown irony, I glared at the passing countryside and reflected on the fact that I was heading for the very place from which Keith Burkinshaw had first fetched Ardiles to London. Despite this marathon journey I resolved there and then to jump on another coach, the first available, south across the Humid Pampas to the seaside resort of Mar del Plata, where I intended getting blind drunk. While I was waiting, that postcard got binned.

Albion supporters who have never forgiven Ossie Ardiles and branded him just another cheating Argie might draw a morbid chuckle from the Malvinas War Memorial, situated in parkland an ironic stone's throw from the replica Big Ben presented to Buenos Aires by the British in 1910. I'd known that his pilot cousin had perished and was bound to seek out his name as I inspected the poignant monument and its lists of fallen, some 650 in all, conferring belated dignity upon tragic pawns whom our own tabloid press had merely dismissed as excrement. Surnames on the left, first names to the right, and there it was: Ardiles Jose Leonidas. Almost surreally, the adjacent first name on the parallel list to the left was...yes. For myself, I shall still always wish Osvaldo Ardiles a long life and the best of fortune within it.

Argentina's humanity is nowhere more touchingly experienced than on each Thursday afternoon in the Plaza de Mayo. Here, as they have done for twenty-odd years, relatives of those who "disappeared" gather together before slowly circling, anti-clockwise, an obelisk in full view of the presidential palace. What began as truly brave defiance nowadays seems more an eternal ritual of mutual comfort, but the root purpose of the protest remains: to prick

The "Mothers of The Disappeared" in the Plaza de Mayo

the powers-that-be into owning up to what happened to their kin after abduction as perceived political opponents by the security forces during those dark, Dirty years. Some estimates put the number of such victims as high as thirty thousand. The Madres, in their symbolic white headscarves, would like to discover exactly when and how, perhaps why, if they suffered torture first, and who by, but their quest for justice seems to me hopeless, particularly as Videla and others were pardoned by President Carlos Menem in late 1990 (although Videla's huge can of worms would be reopened in June 1998 by charges of child theft perpetrated during those days in power). But to see their dignity and warmth, their stoicism and perseverance, is to see an embodiment of souls enriched through dealing with a terrible adversity, and it is a salutary lesson to us all, whoever we are.

You might have known, said the look. I know more now, I thought. Argentina stood in a new light in June 1993. A Boca Juniors pennant even found its way onto my wall. Five years later, as if symbolising the pronounced détente achieved between my government and theirs, it would survive a cruel night in St Etienne, too. Just.

Chapter 2
Bandit Country

Northern Ireland: Newry Town v WBA 9/8/90

The Côte d'Azur had swelteringly invited blissful idleness and, like its motionless palm trees, I'd accepted. The pastis content of an often refilled glass occasionally trickled down my throat while my sun-glassed eyes, having enviously taken in the opulence of my surroundings, trailed through the pages of a glossy paperback annual lying on my pavement table. Years later, this would make curious reading: a hairy Eric Cantona squinted out of the Marseille page; Arsène Wenger did likewise from Monaco's along with Hoddle, Weah and a youthful Emmanuel Petit; the squads of Brest and Caen included Ginola and Rix; and buried among the afterthought pages was the name of Franck Le Boeuf of Laval. I was in Cannes, and as that first Saturday in August drew to its close I would watch the demolition of the home side by an Enzo Scifo-inspired Auxerre, whilst dodging the attentions of a persistent hornet.

Just seven days later I would find myself in a wholly different environment, and a distraught woman would fear she'd never see her husband again.

My connections with Ulster's Troubles were, very tenuously, just two. The first was that I'd paid several visits to Northern Ireland before they erupted, which invested an innocent bemusement in the subsequent turmoil; the second was that a man who would become my brother-in-law, as a corporal in the Royal Tank Regiment, did numerous tours in the province. My own visits had been in school summer holidays with my father, whose accountant's job had involved regular assignments at Lowry's of Belfast over many years and also enabled him to gobble up – whilst they sneered at the efforts of my junior's tools – the local golf courses. The last of those trips for me had been in 1965. Now, with earth's revolution having seen off another quarter of a century, I was setting out again.

Having arrived home from the French Riviera only a matter of hours before and snatched the barest amount of shut-eye, I took the boat train to Holyhead for the Monday night crossing to Dun Laoghaire, my purpose being to follow the Baggies on tour prior to our calamitous 1990–91 season. The ritzy skyline and glitzy waters of Cannes quickly assumed a distant history as my promenade across Dublin's Connolly station became met by an announcement that, due to a bomb scare on the line, the 8am train for Belfast would terminate at Dundalk. A coach was then to deliver me over the border before a waiting train carried me the rest of the way. Not entirely unexpected and, since I was in no hurry, no real inconvenience either. In fact, in its albeit sinister way, I felt it made my reintroduction to the province the more entertaining a process, and other people were equally unperturbed. "Oh, I expect they're up t'their tricks again," remarked one unenlightened pensioner as she made it onto Dundalk's platform. In the home of Harp lager, nobody seemed to be taking any trouble to stay particularly sharp.

A handful of young Italian tourists, however, were soon to haul themselves from their seats and turn around to gawp open-mouthed through the coach's back window. Just into Ulster, past the Brit soldiers at the control zone and on the outskirts of Newry, a burned-out bus bestrode the road, considered to be the most dangerous stretch in the province for security forces and the scene of numerous terrorist strikes. As a representation of twenty years' violent conflict it was a graphic sight indeed, although its everyday property for the coach driver seemed reflected in his choice of radio station. Whilst the wide-eyed Italians slid back somewhat disconcertedly, Marvin Gaye continued to belt out 'I Heard It Through The Grapevine', and furthermore, as I gazed into the fields, I saw a bull merrily boning a cow.

The train waited at the farming village of Poyntzpass, a place I'd never heard of. It looked nondescript to me and my only thought was that it bore a strange name. Its insignificance would be blown away by two masked gunmen in March 1998 when two best friends, one Catholic and one Protestant, were shot in the back of the head as they sat in a bar there. The absence of bigotry in that friendship would be strongly highlighted by leading politicians as a symbol of the peace settlement being vigorously pursued around that time. The area I had just passed through would develop a quite startling significance for myself much sooner.

A number nine bus out of Belfast, past the imposing white mansion of Stormont – where Northern Ireland's parliament had sat until power was transferred to Westminster in 1972, and which would be the 1998 negotiating scene for a historic Good Friday accord – and I duly arrived at my first tour destination, the market-garden town of Newtownards. A major source of Belfast's vegetable consumption, its Huntsman pub retained a few for my own plate, guarded by a Guinness, and then Mick and Pedro breezed in.

Pedro – I never have found out his real name – is a bloke I know through Mick.

In all the years I've known Mick, seaweed hair has covered most of his back, rings have decorated every finger, the tattoo of a naked woman has adorned a forearm, whilst the snout on his demon-joker's face rivals Concorde. But I doubt if his support of our club can be rivalled, because other than a historic tour of China in 1978 I've never known him miss a match at home or abroad. His sneaking out of a Spanish hospital for a few hours, half-dead with sunstroke, has passed into folklore: enough said.

Several regulars arrived at The Huntsman as the afternoon drifted on and the thickly delicious black stuff went down. One in particular, though seeming as highly strung as the liquor's emblem, was loose of tongue to the point of orchestrating the conversation. Louis proudly told us how the pub's football team raised much money for charity. Other locals proudly mentioned that one of Ards' old boys was none other than George Eastham, who'd made his name here alongside his father thirty-five years earlier before joining Newcastle and becoming a landmark players' libber, and that they had a FIFA bigwig for their President in Harry Cavan. Everyone seemed put out that the rise in fortunes of the Republic's team, particularly with the advent of Big Jack, had coincided with a prolonged downturn that saw Northern Ireland, World Cup warriors in 1958 and 1982, now lost in their shadow. I ventured that at least they'd produced probably the second most extravagantly gifted footballer, after a certain Brazilian, in the history of the game. For some reason this topic failed to take hold, which is perhaps just as well. Had it done so, somewhere along the line of ill-fated, underachieving geniuses I should doubtless have gone into overflow about one Laurie Cunningham, despite the fact that everyone by now was half-cut, especially Louis. Louis invited we three to meet up again in Ards' social club after the match.

The striking memory I have of the game is Castlereagh Park's playing surface. True, this was indeed pre-season, and its condition may have been all the more highlighted by a contrast with the somewhat rustic homeliness of its surrounding stands: cowsheds, to be honest. But it looked absolutely superb, just as it had in Eastham's day, a rich testimony he himself paid in his 1964 autobiography *Determined To Win*. Only a few hundred folk bothered to attend it this evening, though, certainly many less than would have watched Reims grace it in the late fifties en route to challenging di Stefano's Real Madrid for the European Cup, or John Charles bestride it in rattling home a friendly hat-trick for Leeds on another day of a distant past.

Amid the warm hospitality of the club Louis, still in determined drinking mode, eventually enquired what was the next fixture on our schedule. Upon being informed, he reassembled himself to advise us that the first thing we

should do upon arrival in Newry was to seek out the police station, where we
could be told "whereabouts not to venture".

Simplistic. Naive. Unrealistic. Such are the scornful dismissals that might beset someone expressing an ironic view that, of all the causes of conflict, one of
them ought not be a system that is surely supposed fundamentally to endow
humans with morality and tolerance, and another should not be that which is
surely supposed fundamentally to help provide practical shape to our lives. So
much for religion and politics. Humans being what we are, we indeed make
these negatively the roots of war and strife. When John Lennon penned 'Imagine', he might as well have co-opted Pol Pot to sit at his piano.

The ancient unrest in Ireland – in existence for over eight hundred years
since Henry II turned his eye to it in 1166; accelerated in 1608, with Ireland's
having ignored the Reformation to remain Roman Catholic, by James I's hand-
ing over of the six counties of Ulster to Protestant farmers from England and
Scotland – has seen varying degrees of intensity. Michael Collins' reward for
bringing about the Anglo-Irish Treaty of 1921 was to be ambushed and receive
a bullet. The Irish Free State he helped to establish left the British Common-
wealth in 1949 to become the Republic. But there are Irish Catholics who want
their Republic to embrace Ulster as its own (many nationalist hardliners might
view Adams and McGuinness to have merely retraced Collins' steps sev-
enty-seven years later); there are Protestant Ulstermen who remain fiercely
loyal to Britain; and there is a bitter Catholic minority in Ulster. Little did Martin Luther know.

Intensity flared from its backburner in the late 1960s with the prime theatre
being the Ulster city of Londonderry. Despite sixty per cent of its population
being of Catholic persuasion, the council dubiously sustained a Protestant
hand. Denied civil rights and, in many cases, employment, the long-oppressed
eventually erupted and when the RUC, viewed by the oppressed as anti-Catho-
lic, failed to maintain order, British troops were reintroduced to the province.
1969 saw the Provisionals split from the Official IRA; 1972 saw Bloody
Sunday; August 1990 saw the island of Ireland as intractable as ever.

The lady taxi driver who ferried us back to our Belfast digs from Bangor
around midnight the day after the Ards game, and the night before the Newry
game, told Mick that he'd be all right there because of the length of his hair. "If
you've got really short hair, you might get some looks." Whilst contemplating
the fact that my hair was really short, I gazed out of my backseat window and
saw armed soldiers nipping from doorway to doorway, their headgear doubtless concealing their really short hair.

The morning television in our room informed us that this was the nineteenth anniversary of the introduction of internment, and that the previous night two vehicles had been hijacked by masked, armed men and set alight in Newry. During Albion's trip to the USA three months earlier Pedro had witnessed a shooting outside his Los Angeles hotel, and he now wondered aloud whether the club's next choice of excursion might take in Kuwait.

Past the Botanic railway station – temporarily closed off and guarded by rifles – we walked further into an otherwise carefree, modern city centre, much pedestrianised, past pavement coffee drinkers, to find the tourist office which would pre-arrange our accommodation in Newry. It seemed we had no alternative but to stay overnight because on the evidence so far there were no late trains or buses to be had. Mick overheard a landlady on the other end of the telephone ask the cheery young girl on the desk: "What are they?" The young girl said: "Foreigners." Mick and Pedro chuckled. I was now beginning to wonder, after Louis's serious concern, the taxi driver's homily, the television news, and now this expression, what the fuck lay in store.

The town of Newry is named from a yew tree said to have been planted by St Patrick himself, and its annals are not without other notable events. It was here in 1578 that Sir Nicholas Bagenal, Grand Marshal of all English forces in Ireland, built the first Protestant church, whilst in 1800 an Act of Union to join the English and Irish parliaments was said to have been drafted a mile and a half away at Derrymore House. Seventy years before that the earliest inland canal in the British Isles, pre-dating the Industrial Revolution, was constructed at Newry.

Sure enough, it was in Canal Street that the taxi dropped us at Mrs Flynn's guesthouse, before we set out to explore. In addition to being situated close to the border with the Republic, the largely Catholic town could barely have come any closer to strongly nationalist southern Armagh: the town hall, curiously resting on a bridge over the River Clanrye, is actually half in County Down and half in Armagh. Nowhere had the armed clash between the Provos and the British Army been more evident than in south Armagh, earning for the area its epithet of IRA 'Bandit Country'. As an ancient frontier town, located at a gap in the mountains separating the plains of Louth from those of Ulster, Newry has historically provided an arena for conflict too, and has seen much activity – of the most brutal sort where "touts" were concerned – over the course of the Troubles.

As we sought out The Showgrounds, Newry Town's little stadium, there were several Republican flags atop telephone poles here and there, and some interestingly artistic murals to be seen. Aside from these, Newry's picturesqueness had immediately struck me, enhanced strongly by the scenic back-drop of the Mourne Mountains. The place possessed charm, no doubt, but to call it romantic would mean to idealise its mystery by ignoring hostility.

Its football team had failed conspicuously to trouble the statisticians since its formation sixty-seven years earlier, reaching no Irish FA Cup Finals and managing at best third place in the league in 1928, even then a distant twelve points behind the champions of Belfast Celtic, a famous old club that dissolved in 1949 because of the sectarian violence. We eventually found the stadium just past a huge Catholic cemetery and industrial estate on the outskirts of town. It wasn't as smart as the Gaelic football ground a couple of hundred yards away, but the green hills that rubbed against it lent a pleasant kind of intimacy to its setting. It was a setting that had launched the stardom of surely one of the finest goalkeepers in football history. Newry Town's chief claim to fame is that none other than Pat Jennings began here.

After the game – buzzed almost surreally as dusk descended by a patrolling army helicopter and, like the Ards encounter, won comfortably by an Albion side that nine months later would shower the club with ignominy – we repaired again to the adjoining bar. Someone told us there that the Newry Town club – management, players, supporters – was roughly fifty-fifty in terms of religious and political persuasion.

There was nothing halfway-house about the bar, though. It was a hive of conviviality, sandwiches laid on, and Newry's Dublin-based goalkeeper Brian O'Shea took the time to come over and not only chat but also stand us a Guinness each – and by this time we were much more than three visitors – which I thought was smashing of him. He told us he'd just taken the opportunity of renewing his acquaintance with Albion's Gary Bannister, with whom he'd been once upon a time at Sheffield Wednesday, where he'd "loved the city but didn't like the training": under Howard Wilkinson.

The sheer niceness of that social club became mirrored in the mother town the following day. If the truth be known, with my obvious accent and really short hair, I did receive the odd quizzing look in the late morning when, while Mick and Pedro lay in, I began my drinking alone. As I ordered at the bar, there was more than an everyday glance, but not after I'd whipped off my jacket to reveal the mere purpose of my presence in the form of an Albion T-shirt. Thereafter the three of us – eventually just Mick and myself as Pedro fell by the wayside – enjoyed a memorable drinking spree that lasted into the small hours. The town was busy – many Southerners, where it's more expensive, cross to shop in Newry (and also stock up with petrol at any of the several fill-ing stations crammed just this side of the border) – and the sunshine made the intermittent strolling in between boozers the more pleasant. With folk ambling around, perhaps enjoying a pub meal, and always the sweeping hills to caress the eye, I could well have been in Buxton. As in Belfast, Newtownards and Bangor, we met civility and out-of-their-way helpfulness. Given that we'd decided to stay a second night, we ended up in a headbangers' disco. I didn't even see any dandruff. Somehow Newry epitomised Ireland's if-onlyness.

So at noon the following day, Saturday, we sat on a coach that waited outside Newry railway station to take us to Dundalk, where we could all rejoin for Dublin the train service that yet again had been disrupted by a bomb alert.

By Friday 22nd May 1998, the day upon which a referendum of the Irish people endorsed the politicians' agreement of Good Friday and led Tony Blair and President Clinton to highly optimistically – jumping the gun, somewhat – declare Northern Ireland's war to be over, around 3,600 people had been killed in Ulster since the Troubles began. Of those, the 13,000-strong Royal Ulster Constabulary – more than ninety per cent Protestant, though IRA intimidation felt by potential Catholic recruits may have had a part to play in that disproportion – had seen 277 of its officers perish.

At around 7.30 pm on Saturday 11th August 1990, a transit van carrying five prison officers and an RUC man back home from a fishing trip in the Irish Republic was stopped by an armed IRA gang at a bogus checkpoint a few hundred yards north of the border, close to Newry. Three of the prison officers managed to run to safety across the fields, but the other three men were seized. Of these, two were later released after being beaten. The remaining victim was the RUC officer, whom the gang had asked for by name at the start.

With still no sign of him six days later, his wife was begging through the media for his return. He needed his tablets for high blood pressure, she said, and he'd undergone treatment over the past three years for severe depression, which had caused him to miss work for much of that time. Police confirmed that the missing man was forty-two years of age, was based in Belfast, and lived in Newtownards.

He was PC Louis Robinson.

Chapter 3
Wan Team in Dejvice

Czechoslovakia: Dukla Prague v Sparta 3/6/92

On a Wednesday evening three weeks before Christmas 1965 I had my first sight of a foreign football team in the flesh, so to speak. And what a team it was. It had been in the hat for the European Cup six times already, which was how its name had become household even for this fourteen-year-old growing up in the East Midlands, carrying a ring still nowadays resonant of those glorious formative years of what we Europeans consider the most prestigious club competition in the world; several of its members had played in the World Cup Final three and a half years earlier; it had surnames to conjure with. There were Novak and Pluskal; there was Jelinek, subject of many an amused self-commentary as fridos bounced off classroom walls; Masopust, the first Eastern player to be voted European Footballer Of The Year; and there was a young goalkeeper called Viktor, who a year later would spectacularly keep a clean sheet at Wembley against the new World Champions. Irritatingly, the weather acceded to Sod's Law, but the difficulty I had in picking out these maestros from the thick mist lent them a kind of spectral quality. The fog also invested in Derby County's decrepit old ground an undeserved grandeur because every now and again I would glimpse what seemed behind the goals to be stands that were very tall, certainly with seats in their upper tiers, unusual indeed in those days. The fact that this was my first ever visit to The Baseball Ground for this floodlit friendly, even though I lived only a few miles away, underlined my allegiance to my chosen team. Three decades later, the famous team I'd come to watch tonight would look ghostly in a much less dreamy way when I saw them next, and even though one and a quarter million folk lived on their doorstep, there would be precious few among that gathering who swore allegiance to them.

That their heyday should have been during a particularly dark period of the former Czechoslovakia's history is no coincidence, and nor is it one that they should have gone into sharp decline in the years following the Velvet Revolution. Dukla Prague: what a case history.

The morning train from Dresden raced alongside the River Elbe through green forested mountains to the passport-stamping town of Děčín, site of a giant castle that served as a Soviet army garrison after the 1968 invasion and had been closed to the public ever since. Inside North Bohemia, as the Elbe became the Labe and dwellings lost colour and opulence, the verdant hills would eventually subside into a flatter landscape, but not before whispering a historical reminder or two. This was part of the Sudetenland, occupied by Nazi Germany in October 1938 with the blessing of Churchill's naively appeasing predecessor, who summed up Czechoslovakia as merely "a faraway country" and its people as "of whom we know nothing" before his precious piece of paper became less triumphally a section of bog roll. After the train had left Lovosice, someone in the next compartment decided to relieve it of a couple of beer bottles. A much stronger arm might have flung them to within dribbling distance of a particular site of Nazi cynicism, a so-called model centre for Jewish internees during

World War Two whose façade convinced the International Red Cross of its accommodating innocence whilst meantime, as a transit camp in reality, it would process over a hundred thousand souls towards the furnaces of, particularly, Auschwitz. There is a sight within a site in Prague that will never leave me. A small museum by the weird Old Jewish Cemetery features sketchings by children concentrated so coldly in Terezín. Some bemused but fearful, skirted and innocent, palpably talented sprog had drawn a cat. The cat's face springs from the exercise book's sheet as if with flesh. I've been to Auschwitz: seen the grey hair, spectacles, suitcases, pots, babies' shoes; and, flesh-creepingly, stood in the original, experimental gas chamber. Auschwitz commemorates the slaughtered through the everyday things they were shorn of. Little Ilona Weissova's drawing commemorates the slaughtered through what they were capable of. People over the years have eulogised the magic of the Mona Lisa. I wonder how many have seen that cat. It's my Holocaust.

The train limped along, as if a law unto itself (unlike the Czech people through much of their history). It opted to rest here and there, before it finally deposited me at Hlavní station more than an hour late: my first visit of Prague. On the approach, high on a hillside, I spied a football stadium: Dukla's.

This was October 1990, almost the anniversary of the bloodless revolution which, as a hauling down of one of the Iron Curtain's hooks, had freed Czechoslovakia of its post-World War Two Soviet yoke into a new era. Though Prague had been occupied during that war, its romantic skyline was largely spared disfigurement – the "city of a hundred spires" – and its centre retained a distinctly medieval feel with its stone palaces, churches and unhurried cobbled streets. Whilst Venice is surely unique, there was an extraordinary timelessness about this place too, and a similarly obstinate one. Italy's jewel contends with the awful threat of submergence; Prague, swallowed by totalitarianism like some gold necklace into the belly of a bear, had emerged to once again breathe afresh and show how unthinkably inappropriate its erstwhile languishing had been. After all, Goethe had once described it as "the prettiest gem in the stone crown of the world".

My first visit was a time of languid uncertainty in the new climate that had seen the former dissident playwright Václav Havel elected President ten months earlier. An American bank, for example, had recently conducted an opinion poll among the people in which eighty-seven per cent had replied that they favoured a market economy, and eighty-five per cent of those same respondents had somehow also stated that they wanted a planned economy. It lent weight to the theory that those who'd dismantled the Communist government hadn't really thought through – or cared about – the consequences.

The one glorious certainty for this English tourist, however, was the availability of ridiculously cheap beer, despite its being recognised as one of the world's best – so good that the Czechs, per capita, do more drinking than any other nation on earth. In a beer hall called U Flekù, six large glasses came to the equivalent of a quid. Stumbling further, as ageing neon signs maintained their espousals of Polish machines and Balkan wines, I came across a grubby, nameless bar the size of a cell, its door thankfully open to the street so as not to be completely missed. The exchange rate at the time was fifty-nine crowns to the pound. A large beer here screwed me for all of three crowns seventy. The cell was chock-full of inmates who looked like habitual offenders.

There was nothing offensive about Prague at this point in time, except when you took up its melancholy invitations to imagine why its face had been so contorted with pain in the past. Less than two years later though, on my second visit, it would present a much different complexion. The fairy-tale would have relinquished much of its magic to the forces of so-called progress. And Dukla, Cup winners in a penalty shoot-out in 1990, would finally have fallen on their own face.

Prague's football stadia are not for the aesthete. With a couple of exceptions, they are purely for the nostalgia-freak. In the days before Glasgow Rangers became tarted up by men in suits, a visit to Ibrox, with a huge open terrace at one end and a roofed one at the other housing probably several psychopaths, invited one to picture this same setting in yesteryear: the raucous hordes baying appreciatively at a Woodburn tackle, a Morton dribble or a McPhail goal. Though doubtless still a citadel, on today's domestic scene anyway, Ibrox seems merely a plushily faceless theatre for the present, its past deeds left entirely to the imagination without the benefit of prompting. Though Prague's grounds would be considered by comfort-seekers to be horrid dumps, their beauty lies, perversely perhaps, in a total lack of pretension which readily recalls a long-ago game that was untouched by commercial inroad. In reality: sorely cash-strapped. In fantasy: wonderfully evocative, particularly for the foreign visitor, overriding any aged physical ugliness.

On the subject of past deeds, Czech football has much to say, and such words would help explain how Dukla were unloved by so many. As the game's sprout flowered in the 1930s – with the World Cup inaugurated and Europe's first cross-nation club competition, Hugo Meisl's Mitropa Cup for Central European teams, enjoying its heyday – Czechoslovakia loudly announced itself. They'd already reached an Olympic Final in 1920 but now, with their close-passing style born of the influence of early Scottish coaches, they progressed all the way to the World Cup Final of 1934. Here, in a bruising match, they eventually succumbed in extra-time to the host nation Italy, but not before they'd made the watching Mussolini squirm by hitting the woodwork when already a goal up. The legendary manager Vittorio Pozzo described his opponents thus: "...for team play, pure combination, it must be said that there were marked periods when the Czech team was superior ...it has a unity and cohesion guaranteed by the fact that the players which form it come from only two clubs: seven men from Slavia and four from Sparta of Prague..." This was the team of Nejedly, the left-winger Puc (whose thirty-four goals for Czechoslovakia were never surpassed), but above all of the captain and goalkeeper Frantisek Planicka: in Pozzo's words "a colossus", and a man who would play nearly one thousand times for Slavia and seventy-three for the national side. It was also a team that in Prague, just prior to that tournament, had inflicted upon England only our fourth defeat at the hands of foreign opposition.

The 1930s were the golden age of Czech football – a powerful national team, and club sides, free then of state manipulation and regularly playing to healthy crowds, making their mark on the international scene too. As the deadly earnest predecessor of the European Cup, the Mitropa Cup was contested variously over the years by the leading teams of Hungary, Austria, Czechoslovakia, Yugoslavia and Italy among others. Sparta twice won it, and Slavia triumphed too. These two were indeed the vanguard of the Czech game that had seen professionalism introduced in 1925, and from that year until 1948 they would monopolise the Championship, Slavia bagging thirteen titles and Sparta nine.

Both had been formed in the same neighbourhood as the nineteenth century drew to its close and their traditional rivalry – in the hearts of generations of their supporters, at least – has, in more than one sense of the word, been as enduring as the city that spawned them. Whilst Sparta has historically drawn its fan base from the working-classes, Slavia was born of perhaps more grandiose stuff. In those days, with the first state of Czechoslovakia not to be established till the end of World War One, Prague was under the Austro-Hungarian Empire. Slavia developed from a Czech-language social association, incorporated within its colours a red star from an independent Czech flag, attracted rebellious support from Prague's intelligentsia, and maintained such an ethos (never mind beyond) for the next half-century. Come the next political upheaval in the wake of World War Two, such bourgeois characterisation would have dire consequences.

The match programme for the European Cup quarter-final second-leg tie at White Hart Lane on February 26th 1962 makes telling reading. For a start, there is an action photograph from the first leg which, because the stadium of that evening's visitors had been of insufficient capacity at that time, was played at "the Dynamo Stadium". For Slavia Prague, a club of such romance, read now – although the same entity – Dynamo Slavia Prague. Tottenham's visitors had sixteen members of their squad pen-pictured: thirteen had been acquired from other clubs. Since Czech football was by now officially amateur again, no transfer fees would have been involved anyway, so there were none to be mentioned. Nor were the words "privilege" or "poaching".

Native dislike of Dukla Prague had its root in two truths: they did indeed take their pick of those players whom they fancied from other Czech clubs; that they were able to do so was because, in bare essence, they were mandated from Moscow.

Once peace was restored after the Second World War, during which Bohemia and Moravia had been an annexed "protectorate" of the occupying Nazis whilst Slovakia had been a separate state, albeit a Nazi puppet one, Czechoslovakia was re-established as an independent state. In early 1948 the Communist party, tired with the frictions of a coalition government, seized total power with the backing of the Soviet Union, and the new government became constituted along Soviet lines. Democracy was thus suffocated by dictatorship, and Czechoslovakia was pulled the dark side of the Iron Curtain as a satellite of the USSR, whose sports ideology – fundamentally a means of glorifying a superior political system and society – was consequently adopted. In the Eastern bloc countries, many football clubs became realigned under the sponsoring umbrella of not only industrial organisations and regional sports clubs but also the security police and the army: convenient for a pretence of amateurism, and very convenient for a few favoured clubs. Dukla was a child of such reorganisation.

Formed only in 1948 as ATK (Army Sports Club) – the Czechoslovakian army, by government decree, was to be given its own team – they became UDA (Central House of the Czech Army) in 1953. They won their first league championship that same year with the aid of the recently enlisted Masopust and Novak from Technomat Teplice, and finally adopted their famous title three years later. Unsurprisingly, this choice of new name recalled a glorious deed already enacted by one body comprising Czechoslovaks and Soviets, and was thus conducive to the purpose of instilling the virtues of serving state and party. The Dukla Pass, on the border of East Slovakia and Poland, had been the site of a protracted battle against the Germans in late 1944 during which 85,000 Soviet soldiers and 6,500 members of Czechoslovak units had either perished or were wounded as the price of victory.

The artificial new club, benefiting from being able to call upon the cream of the country's players as they did their compulsory two-year military service (and who were often induced to stay cushily thereafter), eventually became the dominant force in Czech football. The Championship was theirs seven times between 1956 and 1966. Along the way they moved to a new stadium, the Juliska, in the military district of Dejvice. The Busby Babes lost in Prague in the round before their tragic encounter with Red Star Belgrade. Other European Cup campaigns would see the Spurs team of Blanchflower, Mackay and White forced to pull back a first-leg deficit, Benfica stretched all the way a year later and a third successive quarter-final reached in 1964. In 1967 Anderlecht and Ajax – who'd slaughtered Liverpool 5–1 in Amsterdam – were sent packing as Dukla strode into the semi-final, where they succumbed only to Celtic in their glory year. As the flagship team of Czech football, Dukla would travel the world, notably winning invitational tournaments in New York in 1961, 1962 and 1963. Meanwhile they provided the bedrock of the national side, with Masopust actually giving that the lead in the 1962 World Cup Final against Brazil.

In the meantime poor, bourgeois Slavia were feeling the full scorn of the Communist order, as much under its thumb as Czech culture itself was underground. Starved of resources, denuded of players, they were forced not only to change their name – surely in nothing other than sarcasm, since the Dynamo clubs of the Warsaw Pact countries were usually those of the secret police – but also to see their address renamed Vladivostock Street, as the area sprouted rows of faceless tower blocks. They had slid into the second division in 1951. It would take a long time to climb back, to recover their old name, and even longer for their fans to forgive.

Scorn became heaped upon Czechoslovakia itself somewhat more resoundingly in August 1968 when the Soviet Union, alarmed at the reformist plans of President Alexander Dubček to introduce democracy and end censorship – "socialism with a human face" – sent in 200,000 troops to crush the rebellion and re-establish totalitarian rule. In such an infamous context, it would have been of no consolation whatsoever to the outraged, in many cases suicidal, population, and certainly not to Dubček as he took up his new post at the Slovak forestry department, that the gradual liberalisation process had achieved at least something before the tanks rolled in. In that ill-fated climate of change, the reorganised Czech FA had ruled that players must return to their original clubs after two years' army service at Dukla. This stuck. Dukla Prague would be required to nurture their own players from now on, and their days of supremacy were numbered. The previous two seasons had already seen the Championship land elsewhere. It would be nine years before they won it again; twice more after that, the last in 1982, would be their lot, and they would then have to settle for an odd runners-up spot and Cup success before the rot really set in. And when it did so – unlike in the case of Slavia – hardly anybody cared, except to spit.

Getting digs in June 1992 was awkward and I had to use Pragotur, a travel agency that specialised in finding rooms in private homes, and whose office was ironically situated opposite the tantalisingly luxurious Hotel Paříž. The address was a taxi ride away on the fringes of town, an area of tenement blocks of different hues of brown that could have been in Glasgow decades ago, and still my feet needed to do some wandering and my tongue some asking since the room was proving elusive. Inside one wrong tenement I emerged from the lift, saw no likelihood, so rang any buzzer for help. This immediately set off another sound, one from hell, whose possessor indeed bore a passable resemblance to the star of a silly little film I'd once drunkenly watched one Friday midnight in years gone by. When the door was eventually unbolted, the now growling Zoltan, Hound of Dracula, was being restrained by a man-mountain in a string vest and with enough hairs sprouting from his shoulders to immobilise the whole dark block's sanitary system had he ever reaped and flushed them. Nevertheless, he it was who pointed me at last in the right direction.

The woman was aged around forty-five, polite, had several words of English, a husband and a ten-year-old son, and an unsmiling demeanour and eyes that betrayed a largely wasted life. I'd already seen the shelf-loads of textbooks, but it was only after she'd left that I noticed the framed old photograph which showed her, smiling proudly and widely, in her graduation gown. I did my sums and settled upon the likely year. Her achievement had resulted in her needing to accommodate an arsehole like me.

A couple of hours later, after paying roughly double for beer compared with twenty months ago, except in the case of one establishment that charged forty-five crowns for a single glass of cat's piss, I revisited Wenceslas Square. It was approaching midnight, and most places were closing. Good King Wenceslas, atop his horse, was unavailable for comment, but I know I didn't like what I saw. For a start, at one of the stalls further down Václavské náměstí, the historic street leading up to his statue, I'd presented a bag of scooped toffees for payment: the old hag had demanded 112 crowns. Did these remain in my pocket? A waif with rotten teeth and greasy hair who looked no older than sixteen approached me. "Business? Sex? Machen?" One modern-day expression I hate is "street-wise". It almost seems that merely to wear a baseball cap back-to-front and shirt outside trousers, looking surly, qualifies you. What exactly does it mean, anyway? Why "street"? How "wise"? On this now particularly tacky-looking street, with many seedy, opportunist characters milling around, I felt that I was the wise one because I wasn't buying and I wasn't getting involved. Those around me who doubtless aspired to the new, western "street-wisdom" just looked like wankers to me.

I then revisited something near the base of the statue and felt pleased that it was still loved, with flowers and candles: the memorial to anti-Communist protestors in the wake of the 1968 tanks. It especially commemorated young Jan Palach, who in January 1969 had set himself on fire in this spot and took four days to die. The solemnity of this shrine was now being pummelled by the blaring beat and flashing lights of a disco within staggering distance. I told myself that this was what Jan would have wanted, and I felt I was thinking the truth.

The following morning I again strolled, like all the other countless tourists do, along the 600-year-old Charles' Bridge spanning the silent storyteller that is the Vltava river. Pedestrianised for the past twenty-odd years, it was now less a thoroughfare than a sideshow with stallholders, souvenir-pedlars, street-artists and buskers, not to mention moneychangers and pickpockets. As the waters dawdled beneath and the special panorama enticed, palaces, towers and steeples amid the russet roofs, the bridge itself seemed just a cliché, especially with long blond-haired, bearded Americans wailing on about their long-lost dreams as their guitars eroded a few more bricks.

Prague had become beset by grockles and cardsharps, and by people – especially American – with an entrepreneurial eye for the main chance. Although it was now opportunistically more expensive than before, it was cheaper, and spoilt: for me, that is, compared with October 1990. I felt thankful, anyway, that I'd already been before it was too late, when a whole new daybreak brought a wonder that was innocent and uncluttered. With such thoughts of new dawns and horizons, I made my way to Dejvice.

Instead of fog, there was torrential rain as I approached this surprisingly pleasant area on Prague's north-western outskirts, close to a nature park and a historic seventeenth-century battle site. Greenery and steep roads surrounded the 28,000-capacity Juliska Stadium, part of which was carved out of a hillside that also provided a leafy abode for none other than Emil Zatopek, legendary Olympian from 1952 when a member of the multi-sport ATK club, but stripped of everything including his passport for facing the tanks sixteen years later, and demoted from army colonel to civic roadsweeper.

The melee outside and late rush to get in were caused by the curiously late Wednesday afternoon kick-off hour which gave the fans precious little time to get there from work. Several, young and old, simply clambered brazenly over the fences without challenge. After paying the princely admission fee of twenty-five pence I discovered that the game had been delayed anyway, either to let the heavenburst subside, to let everyone in for the start, or both. I also discovered that, for all the mad scramble, the place was nevertheless only a quarter full, with virtually everyone making for the only cover provided by the vast, 11,000-capacity grandstand-in-the-hill. I duly joined them, hauled myself to the very top, surveyed the scene, and realised that I'd come across another example of Prague's eccentric stadia. At least this one just about had four sides. Slavia's ground, affectionately known as Eden, had but three on my earlier tour. Sitting in the old wooden stand there with its "Don't Forget Bradford" no-smoking signs, I'd had a choice of a bleak high-rise estate to my left and a grimy railway track to my right to look at over the open, decaying terracing, but nothing save advertising boards and a huge weeping willow beyond its far touchline.

It almost seemed, with Dukla having caught a cold over the years, that the huge stand had let out an almighty, inharmonious sneeze to blow most of the rest away, so disproportionate was the place. Opposite was a shallow terrace with, on the halfway line, a weird old double balcony on stilts the width of a goal area. Beyond, past a brewery, a hotel designed to look like some giant syringe, and several conifers, was perhaps some pleasantly panoramic view, but right now with the weather so unseasonably gloomy and wet that the floodlights soon came on, this was hiding. To the right were merely club buildings. To the left, with more uniform Moscow-bred rows of tower blocks just visible on high in the distance, was more shallow terracing. The overall effect from where I stood at the back, if I ignored the people in front and the various rubble and tools behind, was akin to peering out from a top floor hotel balcony onto some little amateur club ground below, athletics track or not.

"Please score a goal! Please score a goal!" chanted – yes, indeed, in an English of sorts – a small gathering of denim-clad yobs braving the elements down there on the left, when the game had got going. They, like just about everybody else here, had come in hope of an away victory on this final day of the league season. "Vitkovice! Vitkovice!" was often another airing, as was, with rather less linguistic charm, "Hooligans! Hooligans!" A miraculous Vitkovice win at Slovan Bratislava and a simultaneous defeat for Dukla was the only formula that would bring the visitors the championship. The visitors were Sparta, who'd had a much less agonising time of it than Slavia during the Communist years and more recently had, indeed, won seven of the last eight titles.

The pitch, apart from being waterlogged, looked to me bigger than most and upon it the game was an open one with several nice touches despite the conditions. Sparta, unsurprisingly, looked strong and confident – Jozef Chovanec, not long back from PSV Eindhoven, lived up to his star billing – but Dukla's part really was nothing else than a bit one. Nevertheless, as word circulated of Slovan's elsewhere stroll and the exercise took on an increasingly futile nature, the former masters managed to take the lead with ten minutes left, a glancing header from a left-wing cross. Within sixty seconds Sparta capitalised upon some ludicrous defending to equalise, also from close range. And that was that; while Slovan triumphed 3–0.

I'd heard of none of Dukla's players. The distinctive heavy red had disappeared from their colours which were now an everyday all-yellow. I'd neither seen a single emblem nor heard a single voice in their support. The Juliska had merely served as an assembly point for domineering visitors, like some rebuking echo of Eden's being used for that Tottenham tie in yesterdecade. Was this the pitch that Josef Masopust had bestrode? That Jock Stein had sat alongside willing his Celtic team to survive to face Inter Milan? The home of a team that had captured the imagination of my boyhood? The team was entirely irrelevant, for the club was an afterbirth. In its impotence, its new innocence, it was today still a Prague misfit.

Much worse would follow. Two years later, by which time federal Czechoslovakia had peacefully split into two separate nations and the army of the new Czech Republic had withdrawn its support of the club, Dukla were relegated to the second division then immediately sank into the technically amateur, regional third.

And yet by July 1997 – by when the national team, almost poetically containing six past or present players from the strongly resurgent Slavia and four from Sparta, had gone within a whisker of repeating the Slovak-led 1976 European Championship triumph, and in which month the Czech Republic was invited to become a full member of NATO – they were back in the top flight, courtesy mainly of indeed a cute entrepreneur. Not at Dejvice, though. Dukla now played outside Prague, at little Pribram. Their phoenix-like recovery also saw them reach the Cup Final that year: but lose to grand old Slavia, soon to become part of the expansive portfolio of ENIC, an investment company backed by a Bahamas-based billionaire, which will not stem the inevitable flow of Czech players seeking fortunes elsewhere but may assist towards a renewed growth in the game of one of football's historically admired peoples.

History. If football were a library, that would still be Dukla's shelf. A club that once upon a time flourished through the favourable gerrymandering of a seemingly immovable power, when European football was played upon a commercially level field. How times can change. But can Dukla Prague ever be popular?

Chapter 4

Simply Red

Portugal: Benfica v Sporting Lisbon 30/4/95

A West German numskull was to blame in 1971 when his Coca-Cola can struck Roberto Boninsegna's head and, upon the Italians' appeal, Borussia Moenchengladbach's 7–1 European Cup annihilation of Inter Milan was erased from the record. Spuriously, Inter would progress to the next round. Ten years earlier torrential rain had been the culprit at Kenilworth Road when Luton's FA Cup tie against Manchester City was knocked on the head after seventy minutes and Denis Law's six goals were annulled. Curiously, Luton would progress to the next round. More recently, in April 1994, the German Football Federation – courageously of spirit, dangerously in precedent – acted upon television evidence that showed title-chasing Bayern Munich's winning goal to have struck relegation-battling Nuremberg's net from the wrong side of an upright, and ordered the crucial game to be played all over again. Bayern would now win furiously, 5–0, secure the championship, and Nuremberg would drop.

A year after that I would witness another referee's moment of aberration, not a singular incident but the climax of his escalating confusion, resulting in yet another case (and fans of Arsenal and Sheffield United will know the feeling) of some match that never was.

The small Algarve town of Lagos possesses a vast beach, weirdly wonderful rock formations, a tangle of narrow cobbled streets, and a glut of bars and restaurants. In late spring, prior to the boisterousness of the high season, its ambience provides a very agreeable holiday spot. It is also significantly historic, although architectural evidence of this is thin, since its downfall as the Algarve's capital had been literal when a devastating earthquake struck in the mid-18th century. From Lagos, inspired by Prince Henry the Navigator, had set sail many of the early voyages that heralded Portugal's Age of Discoveries. Less honourably, in 1444, it was where black Africans were first sold as slaves to Europeans. Catastrophically, in 1578, King Sebastião left here with an army of 18,000 that included most of the nation's nobility in an attempt to impose Christianity upon Morocco, and got slaughtered, a mess that led to Portugal's

Lisbon skyline and the Tagus estuary

loss of independence to Spain. There stands – or rather, teeters, looking for all the world like some bewildered flowerpotman – a howlingly risible statue of Sebastião in the town's Gil Eames square. The Moors could only have slain him after first pissing themselves at the sight of what was stepping from the ship. Just off the square, in Veejay's, the barman wasn't laughing as he bemoaned other sales of humanity as a symptom of his beloved Benfica's decline.

The strange case of Paulo Futre a couple of years earlier had highlighted the parlous state into which the club had sunk. One of the most gifted European forwards of his generation, though sadly injury-prone and temperamental, Benfica had paid Atletico Madrid £4.5 million for him. Within five months he'd departed, complaining that his pay cheques had bounced. It also transpired that of the cash with which he'd been bought, £3 million had been provided by the Portuguese state TV network – public money, resulting in furious protests from Benfica's rivals and a television boss losing his job. Futre hadn't been the only one missing his salary: among several others was midfielder Paulo Sousa, who promptly decamped to none other than arch-enemies Sporting. That Benfica – a national multi-sport institution that had transcended monarchy, dictatorship and democracy, and whose football team within the previous five years had added two more to its long list of European Cup Final appearances – were now sorely cash-strapped, was emphasised when the construction company that had enlarged their stadium threatened to sue for a £2.2 million payment still outstanding. The club had to resort to asking for donations to help lessen their debts, estimated at £4.5 million, much of this owed to the taxman. Subsequently their predicament had somewhat eased, and when the *socios* – fee-paying members who essentially owned Benfica, and whose numbers had now swelled in excess of a hundred thousand – elected a new President, Manuel Damasio, he emotionally declared, "Benfica deserves everything! Everything!"

João, the barman, saw nothing but depreciation though. "Always leave! Never grow!" he lamented into the early evening. The new President, understandably, had imposed a strict budget upon the new coach. "Already the coach has to tell nine of the players that they must go at the end of the season! Do you think that these men will now play with heart?" The new coach, Artur Jorge, had been appointed the previous summer even though his predecessor, Toni, had just delivered the Championship. Despite that success, the same close-season had seen Benfica forced to sell the gifted Rui Costa to Fiorentina and the influential Stefan Schwarz to Arsenal. "Our driving force driven away!" Still now in a financial mire, the club had recently appealed against a court order that its very headquarters building be sequestrated. Much of the nation found these problems bewildering and disturbing; João was not alone. A poll had found that 88% of the population considered themselves football fans and of these 40% swore allegiance to Benfica. "I don't like Artur Jorge either," said João. "I wish we still had Toni."

Without realising it, João was something of a living emblem of the club. Under a cloud now, he'd been born thirty-five years earlier: around the same time that Benfica had announced themselves to the world too, unfanciedly defeating Barcelona to win the 1961 European Cup, the first team to break Real Madrid's monopoly. The captain of that side, centre-forward Jose Aguas, had been born in Angola; so had João, who'd lived there till the age of fifteen, when independence bloodily tore that country apart. And much of Benfica's success in the 1960s had owed a great deal to those players brought over from Portugal's African colonies.

Lagos had provided a haven – if a frustrating one – for the greatest of those, someone whom the club had never needed to sell, who'd never really wanted to leave anyway, and who became as synonymous with his adopted land as Henry himself.

When Eusébio, from a family of eight fatherless kids in the ramshackle native quarter of Lourenço Marques and a month short of his nineteenth birthday, emerged from his first ever flight, he was alone and nervous. Shivering too, for Lisbon airport towards midnight on 17th December 1960 inflicted an unknown chill. Little did he know that this grand adventure would bring not only immense personal fame and fortune but also unknown respectability to Portugal's international footballing status. Before such wheels could roll, though, the limousine had to be brought out of neutral. Whilst he was met and taken care of within minutes by club officials, it would be five long months before he became legally a Benfica player. Not only was his local club back in Mozambique loath to release him, but rivals Sporting were also striving to grab him instead. Eventually, Benfica thus despatched him to Lagos, out of reach to predatory agents and persuaders, until a deal was completed.

His impact was immediate and sensational. Within five more months, he would hit the bar twice at Wembley in a World Cup qualifier, his second game for Portugal, having scored on his debut. Little more than six months later he would score twice as Benfica defeated Real Madrid 5–3 to retain the European Cup, and, as a mere twenty-year-old, admit that collecting di Stefano's shirt gave him as much pleasure as anything. This persona, one of humility and sheer joy in playing, seemed never lost through all the acclaim. Less than three years after weeping goodbye to his mother he represented FIFA in a match to mark the English FA's Centenary, taking his place in a Rest of the World team alongside Yashin, Masopust, Kopa and di Stefano himself. In 1965 he was voted European Footballer of the Year and in 1966 he was top goalscorer in the World Cup Finals. Two years after that his sportsmanship manifested itself in another European Cup Final – his fourth – when, having been denied a winning goal in the dying moments of normal time, he immediately approached Alex Stepney to offer a handshake of admiration.

By any yardstick Eusébio's achievements, so soon, were phenomenal. They were inextricably linked to, and vital for, the consolidation of Benfica as a major power following their triumph over Barcelona. With Benfica's providing the majority of the national side – including another celebrated black performer from Mozambique, Mario Coluña – Portugal itself could now at last compete with the best. In 1947 England had demolished them 10–0 in Lisbon. The World Cup semi-final of 1966 was a close-run thing. The athleticism, improvisation and sheer technical ability of the African influx – and above all, Eusébio's electrifying bursts, consummate ball control and explosive shooting – had enabled that progress.

Those Benfica and Portugal teams of the sixties were admired particularly because, in an age of increasing negativity, they were enterprising, fluent and stylish. It was indeed their golden era, whose level has yet to be regained, for all that Porto lifted the European Cup in 1987 and lesser Benfica sides lost the

Finals of 1988 and 1990. Only once more, in 1986, has the national team reached the World Cup Finals, where it failed in Mexico. Just three times has it qualified for the final stages of the European Championships. For a nation that continually produces talented performers (though not consistent, reliable goalscorers) – the FIFA World Youth Cup for under-20s was won in both 1989 and 1991 – such meagre attainments at senior level represent a wretched return and fall from grace.

The train from Lagos to Lisbon can run no further than Barreiro station, from whose pier a half-hour ferry ride carries you across the expansive mouth of the River Tagus to its northern bank, beyond which Portugal's capital sits snugly upon its seven hills, pastel shades to the fore. As a form of approaching a destination this is among the nicest, churning waters churning expectation as perhaps the most pleasant city in Europe awaits: "the princess of the world.... before whom even the ocean bows," according to the 16th-century poet Luis Vaz de Camões.

That eulogy is a poignant one because much of what Camões had admired – and much of southern Portugal – was destroyed by the massive earthquake of 1755: Lisbon was shattered by a trio of colossal tremors, set aflame, and then swamped by the angry Tagus. You always hurt the one you love.

But Europe's westernmost capital had repaired itself and, as if in reward, was spared disfigurement by several processes that subsequently shaped much of the continent, being untouched by the Industrial Revolution and uninvolved militarily in World War Two. Though its political climate has suffered instability, and repression under the long Salazar régime, membership of the European Union in 1986 brought means of revitalisation and in 1994 Lisbon stood proud as the European City of Culture. Four years after that it would stage Expo '98, too.

A haul up the bizarre, wrought-iron Elevador de Santa Justa resulted in spectacular views. To the south, distant beyond the main commercial thrust of Baixa and across the estuary on the Setúbal peninsula, loomed a giant statue of Christ with arms outstretched, a smaller model of Rio de Janeiro's. To the east, beyond white walls and red-brown roofs, stood guard the ancient battlements of St George's Castle, dating back to the fifth century, variously a Moorish citadel, a royal palace, and an infamous gaol. To the north, the direction in which headed a long, noisy (and early) column of Sporting fans in the Sunday afternoon sunshine, and beyond a relaxed skyline entered by grander architecture and intermingling greenery, probed the wide Avenida da Liberdade. The Bairro Alto district nestled to the west, accessible by funicular railway, an atmospheric old warren where cramped dwellings and the yellings of nightlife fuse into the city's soul. The following evening, after a daytime tram further west to the stately riverside suburb of Belém with its grand memorials to the great explorers – Vasco da Gama embarked from here in 1497 to find a sea route to India, and is entombed in its magnificent Jerónimos monastery – I would sample those spirited bars of Bairro Alto. Entering one, coughing, to be immediately ordered to hush: to respect the fado, Portugal's very own brand of the blues, where a guitar-backed soloist harrowingly wails out mournful tales of life's heartaches. There is tourist fado and then there is genuine fado, expressed by anyone so driven from bashfulness by an emptying wine bottle, and that soulster is dutifully heeded. I would feel guilty at my intrusion.

Right now, though, I was about to follow those clamorous Sporting Lisbon supporters.

If the name 'Benfica' strikes some magical chord, the façade of the Estádio da Luz hit me straight between the eyes as I emerged from the metro-linked subway. Not so much the realisation that I'd arrived at the home of a legend, nor the imposing, white concrete structure itself; there to greet me, mounted above the plush entrance and immediately visible in its dominance, was a gargantuan sculpted eagle. Although the impoverished club didn't rule the roost nowadays, this bird of prey looked indomitable and positively fearsome. "E Pluribus Unum" – "All For One And One For All" – was the motto inscribed beneath, seemingly announced by the bellicose biped. Whatever you say, I thought.

Another chiselled form nearby, however, left something to be desired. Though the face was instantly recognisable – African, unsullied and endearing – the torso and legs of the statue were inaccurately more bantamweight than the powerhouse that Eusébio had been. A pity. Then again, albeit on a smaller scale, it was a much better effort than the tacky assembly mounted back home in Birmingham's Centenary Square, said to have been inspired by the Discoveries Monument in Belém. Whilst the latter, a caravel in limestone upon which Henry and the rest stand confronting mysteries beyond the waters, appropriately possesses a stylish grandeur, Brum's Forward statue elicits a vague impression of some huge, masticated prawn cracker. A small place is the world nowadays, though, something of which I am constantly reminded by another man-made construction in the West Midlands: the 448 bus to West Bromwich trundles past a scruffy canal into which once descended, at the wheel of his car, a man who would actually come to manage, no less, Benfica. I fondly remembered Jimmy Hagan as I parked myself in sector 36 of the bancada lateral's second tier.

Subsequently absolving Sunderland of plagiarism, the Stadium of Light had by now officially retitled itself the Estádio do Sport Lisboa e Benfica, a much less inspiring appellation, for all that Luz had referred merely to the district in which it stood. Also uninspiring was the attendance tonight. Whereas its three roofless tiers of mostly concrete benches forming Europe's largest football venue had, for example, enabled a capacity 120,000 crowd to celebrate Portugal's World Youth Cup Final victory over Brazil four years earlier, they were now barely a quarter full, reflecting the disenchantment felt by both sets of fans at their teams' fading campaigns.

According to João the Benfica-nut barman, the previous month's defeat by Milan in the European Cup quarter-final had killed the season. Out of touch already in the title race, Benfica had then suffered a knock-out in the Portuguese Cup too, at the hands of bottom club Setúbal. A place in the following season's UEFA Cup was there to be looked forward to, but that was scant consolation and nor would it be as financially rewarding as another much needed tilt at the Champions' League. Still, there was at least the matter of civic pride. Benfica had proved virtually invincible over the past forty years at home to Sporting, and now was an opportunity to not only emphasise this parochial impregnability – their stadia lie merely a mile apart – but also finally abort their rivals' own hopeful chase of Porto for the Championship.

Earlier that season, despite having unloaded players of their own such as Paulo Sousa – to Juventus – Jorge Cadete and the Dutch defender Stan Valckx, Sporting had looked set fair to annex their first title since the double-winning year of 1982 under Malcolm Allison. The feeling had been that Benfica might indeed be preoccupied with the European Cup and that Porto might need time to assimilate Bobby Robson, controversially sacked by themselves midway through the previous season. Sure enough, back in November, Sporting had sat top of the pile; but destiny had forsaken them, and they currently trailed a revamped Porto – inspired by Emerson, later to flirt with Middlesbrough – by five points (two for a win) with five matches remaining, Benfica being eight points further worse off in third place. Ever was it thus. An extraordinary fact of Portuguese football is that since the inception of its Championship in 1935 only once has it been won by a team other than these three, and indeed it had been unusual for any other side to finish higher than fourth.

Also extraordinary was the sight of a live eagle being paraded around the pitch prior to the kick-off! Selhurst Park this wasn't. And then, as the red smoke from the Benfica mob to my right dissipated amid much spluttering and relocating of scarves from mouths to necks, the referee blew for the action to start. At least he managed to get that bit right.

Sporting had beaten Benfica 1–0 on their own turf and here, to the unbridled joy of the green-and-white at that end, they found the net twice within the opening twelve minutes. Michel Preud'Homme had impressed in goal for Belgium during USA '94 but now, in the ninth minute, he probably wished he were still there. Yards out and attempting to work the ball upfield, he succeeded only in scuffing it to Krasimir Balakov, who'd also shone in those World Cup Finals and indeed had earned a place in the FIFA technical commission's select eleven. It was an error akin to leaving home with the keys still in your front door, and with a precise chip from the left corner of the penalty-area, the Bulgarian duly burgled the opener. When his compatriot Ivailo Yordanov danced forward unchallenged to scorch home a twenty-yarder three minutes later, red-and-white was as shocked as the resident history book was mocked. Worse followed. Six minutes more and João Pinto, centre-forward for Benfica and Portugal, collided crunchingly with Sporting's goalkeeper Costinha and was stretchered away. In the meantime the referee, Jorge Coroado, had issued his first yellow card to Benfica's Tavares, despite the fact he'd provided some of the nicest tunes in those days when discos used to play them.

Soon after João Pinto's departure, in the 23rd minute, the impressive full-back Dimas – who would also be bought by Juventus – nipped in at the near post for Paulo Bento's left-wing cross to reduce the arrears. This provoked the stadium announcer to impersonate countless Brazilian television commentators, as the white-suited Eusébio himself performed a delirious jig down by the benches. That concluded the scoring. The less celebratory fun would now unfold.

It was a match both fractious and fragmented. Often splendid technique was confronted by highly physical – typically 'derby' – challenge and, consequently, histrionics. These exacerbated the other and fanned the increasing ire of each set of partisans. Coroado simply couldn't handle it, making everything worse still.

João Pinto's substitution had already been the third due to injury. Four more yellow cards would be brandished by half-time, within a ten-minute spell. Coroado, having failed to control the mood, was now merely reactive to what he'd allowed loose. His now punitive stance became increasingly wobbly and flustered, redolent of those ill-programmed robots whom FIFA had ordered to strut around USA '94, who'd succeeded only in spoiling the fluency of our great game – and the pinnacle of players' careers – and in making rods for their own backs. Robots may assist towards ironing out inconsistency, that perennial lament of players and managers, but they fail to allow for the spirit of this most hyperactive and emotional of sports.

Benfica playing Sporting, eleven-a-side at this point

The day when football becomes basketball watched by a tennis crowd will be the day when football's guardians finally succeed in extinguishing its soul. This balmy night in Lisbon cried out for a Gordon Hill. Instead, Coroado wielded that rod, wholly unconvincingly.

Sporting's Moroccan defender Naybet was the first real casualty. His dismissal after seventy-five minutes for two yellow cards came just two minutes after Benfica's captain Veloso had been likewise sent off. Naybet's transgression had warranted no more than a free-kick but Coroado had snatched at a chance to even matters. In the fifteen minutes between Naybet's two cards he'd also waved yellow at three other Sporting players.

The most wronged victim of this agitated árbitro, though, was someone who'd not only managed to remain clean of his brandishing for eighty-one minutes, but had also been one of the contest's most eye-catching performers. He had also been hardworking in a way that would have cheered the barman, even though he was off to Boca Juniors shortly. One of those poor souls bitterly denied a role in a World Cup Final through suspension, he'd come to prominence in the eyes of many European fans during the opening game of that Italia '90 tournament, when a third Cameroon player had brutally – if entertainingly – succeeded where the previous two had just failed, this now staggering Argentinian finally being whacked into a spiral, kit components joining sparks in the orbit. Claudio Caniggia did nothing violent himself now. A melee by the touchline saw him drag Sporting's volatile Sá Pinto away from the arguments. As Coroado meanwhile attempted to deal with the affray, he missed Sá Pinto's spiteful reaction behind his back, but turned round to see Caniggia now grappling with someone who two years later would earn notoriety for punching the national coach, one Artur Jorge. Whilst Sá Pinto would receive a yellow card, Coroado now showed Caniggia and everyone else just how much he'd lost the plot. He waved a first yellow at Claudio. Then he immediately flourished a red. Caniggia eventually trudged off, nonplussed.

The final minutes would ebb away without incident, Benfica's demoralised nine men reluctant to continue stretching forward for salvage and Sporting's ten content. Through police shields glinting in the now floodlit, draining stadium, Coroado disappeared down the tunnel. As a further indignity, Caniggia – who'd already served a lengthy ban after testing positive for cocaine two years earlier at Roma – was ironically one of four now required to provide a urine sample. He doubtless felt like providing an additive to someone's refreshment.

Back in December at the José Alvalade stadium, this confrontation had produced ten yellows and two reds. Fourteen yellows and three reds here thus eclipsed even that. One of them – bluntly put by the daily sports paper *Record* as "uma estúpida expulsão" – would refuse to go away.

Senhor Coroado was ushered away all right, though his heavy guard had to negotiate a path through a catcalling 500-strong mob of Benfica supporters hanging around afterwards. This vociferous venting of displeasure not only targeted anyone emerging from beneath the giant eagle but also involved several better (and older) managers than Artur Jorge proclaiming where the team was going wrong. Speaker's Corner here would become hustings there, too, as several better (and older) presidents than Damasio set out their remedies. At one point, with the clock by now approaching eleven-thirty at night, I became personally subjected to a whole minute's animated statement, the septuagenarian candidate mistakenly assuming agreement in my silence, unaware that he was spouting forth to a not wholly comprehending Brummie Road-Ender from Bartley Green. Nevertheless, the atmosphere typically carried no menace, and the toleration of the bancada lateral where green and red had mingled was also evident in the streets and on the metro. It was therefore with amazement and dismay that I subsequently learned the unfortunate Caniggia – whose name had been often chanted during the match – was attacked by Benfica fans who'd surrounded his car in a narrow street.

The following weekend Sporting, now only four points adrift, faced Porto, and lost 0–1: a sweetly decisive triumph for Robson, though the occasion was marred by a railings collapse inside the Alvalade that killed one home fan and

Sousa Cintra eufórico com a vitória do Sporting

Não digo que vamos ser campeões mas as esperanças estão intactas

● O líder leonino mostrou-se estupefacto ao saber que o Benfica iria recorrer, alegando um erro de Jorge Coroado. "O Sporting é que tem razões da arbitragem", frisou, sendo corroborado por Costa

FILOMENA MARTINS

A alegria de Sousa Cintra espelhava de forma perfeita o sentimento que a equipa leonina viveu ontem após a vitória no Estádio da Luz, um feito que não obtinha desde 1986. O presidente sportinguista, que entrara no recinto encarnado quase -à Hollywood- — sete minutos antes do jogo, sob escolta de polícias, com sirenes a apitar —, saiu da Luz debaixo de vaias e apupos, com o carro pontapeado, depois de se desdobrar em entrevistas e abraços, sempre ...

Cintra, para quem o título seria a concretização de um sonho. "Pelo que o Sporting fez nos últimos anos merece ser campeão, e a Portugal faz falta o título leonino" A concluir, Cintra falou ainda do -caso Paulo Sousa-, considerando o assunto "ridículo" "O juiz que penalizou o Sporting na anterior delibe ração foi o mesmo que apreciou agora o recurso, o que é contra a lei. Os tribunais comuns vão resolver esse assunto"

Costa e M. Aurélio

Costa, que usou da palavra quando todos espe ravam por Queiroz fala, também em erros na arbi

Newspaper extract describing the controversial sending-off of Caniggia

seriously injured twenty-five others. Sporting would find consolation for their unfruitful league campaign by lifting the Cup, their first major trophy for thirteen years: but lose among others Balakov to Stuttgart and, maintaining the seepage of native talent out of the country, Luis Figo to Barcelona.

As for once-great Benfica themselves, sadly they would merely continue lurching along. Three years later, still subjected to numerous court actions, their bank accounts would be frozen, and another president would need to explain why cheques in payment for Karel Poborsky from Manchester United and Brian Deane from Sheffield United had bounced. Near-bankruptcy provided a clue.

Crises aside, they at least achieved a result back in mid-1995, though again this flew in the face of the doctrine that, idiot or not, the referee's decision is final. On the grounds that Caniggia's sending-off for one yellow card was unlawful, Benfica appealed to the Federation demanding that the match be replayed. The Federation assented, and thus wiped off Sporting's quite historic victory.

On Sunday 18th June the two teams took to the Stadium of Light again. Guess what? Benfica won 2–0.

Chapter 5
Going Dutch

Netherlands: Ajax v AZ '67 Alkmaar 24/2/80

"The biggest fast ferry in the world": that's how Stena Line describes its HSS model. Sailings nowadays from Harwich to Holland halve the old eight-hour marathon, which is marvellously convenient if you can catch the morning crossing. If, however, you take the evening one, you could do with this big ferry being not so fast, for options at the Hook at midnight are minimal, and arrival in Amsterdam at 02.14 is virtually inescapable. With no digs, this presents no favours. For a start, you're prey to all the drug-pushers, fleecers, beggars and nocturnal ne'er-do-wells who inhabit the Centraal station and its environs. I'd previously resolved never to subject myself to such a situation again. So, in the early hours of a Tuesday in March 1999 here I was, heavy bag over right shoulder, consciously beating off unsteadiness and its invitations. I was heading for North Holland province, Alkmaar, but transport was hours away yet and right now I'd nowhere to go. Sod it. What else? I crossed Stationsplein, and turned left off Damrak into the red-light area where, despite the near-deserted streets, bars would still be serving. Mercifully without being accosted, I soon sat on a stool surrounded by several people even more worse for wear, one of whom was Anna, who repeated in slurred half-English that she'd been a survivor of the camps inside the womb of her Jewish mother. The bar closed. So had my sense of bearing. Youths loitered across the bridges. Then I heard voices behind me, approaching very quickly. More shady opportunists? Before I could alarmedly turn round, I was hit by a Dutch idiosyncrasy. Two men on bicycles cruised past me. Suddenly I felt not so adrift after all. Back on Stationsplein, though, I had to emphasise to a baseball cap that I didn't do drugs and convince a skinhead Scouser that I was skint myself and didn't do fags. I grabbed a train to Utrecht. Then I took one back to Amsterdam. Daylight was by now only a few unkilled ticks away, and so was my train northward. On this one I slept. Den Helder, the tip of North Holland, from where wild green islands string closely through the Waddenzee and then German waters as the North European Plain reaches for Scandinavia, jerked me back to life with a screech of brakes. Now I could really make tracks, back, to my destination.

The polder landscape during this final half-hour leg did two things. Its endlessly flat rurality, a kinetic watercolour, tried to deny that The Netherlands is perhaps surprisingly the most densely populated country in Europe. Such a view from the train window also invited daydream, and I reflected upon several visits made many years earlier, when I witnessed the silly rise of copycat hooliganism but, particularly, the ascent of AZ '67 Alkmaar.

Real supporters follow their team bodily week in week out, have the badge engraved on their heart, live the bitterness and occasional sweetness through being there, and take those emotions out of the stadium with them. They can easily find in their hearts contempt for those who claim to be supporters, particularly of fashionable clubs, who neither make any attempt to be there nor can appreciate tradition. I'm not an AZ supporter. I merely have a soft spot somewhere for them, as I do for other teams in other countries for a variety of reasons: Boca Juniors because of the carefree vibrancy I experienced in their heartland; Iraklis because of the ardent, face-screwing passion of their supporters; Bologna because of genuine sadness at their near-demise having seen them illuminate The Hawthorns back in my schooldays. Then there's Malmö, where a sexual paradise – her own word, thank you – shared in Mallorca became unforgettably recreated several times subsequently. My soft spot for AZ, though, grew from admiration of their brand of football back in the late-seventies.

I first saw them at Sparta Rotterdam in October 1975, a mid-table affair ending 1–1 where the names of the players meant nothing to me. The only real impression on this, my introduction to domestic Dutch football, was the overall lack of pulse, passive spectators in a smallish ground left unstirred by unspectacular play on a Sunday afternoon that was leisurely an ocean away from an Anfield Saturday. With the odd exception – usually when Ajax or Feyenoord were concerned – this was generally the case, and locals would tell how they derived enormous pleasure from watching English football on television because of its drive, goalmouth incident and background fervour. By this time, of course, the Dutch national side was something different. And AZ were in the process of so becoming, too.

Their seminal moment had arrived in 1973, six years after Alkmaar '54 merged with FC Zaanstreek to form AZ '67, the new club, which had merely continued along the wholly unsuccessful lines of its forebears, including time spent out of the top division. Two millionaire brothers, Klaas and Kees Molenaar, then took it over, immediately proclaimed their lofty ambition and, to the envy of all the other also-rans, set about bankrolling the process of fulfilment. And on the day I next saw them, in February 1977, there were names that certainly did mean something – plus some that would come to do so – as AZ turned on the style.

The neat little stadium of Twente Enschede, in eastern Holland very close to the German border, was the venue, home of a team that had reached the UEFA Cup Final two years previously, though their performance this day seemed an attempt to refute that. After an initial twenty minutes of untidy wrestling for domination, they were distinctly ineffectual as second fiddle to an AZ outfit whose firm control, based upon coherent teamwork, sound individual technique and the doctrine that possession is nine-tenths of the law, saw them dictate the pace of the game and its outcome. Only in the final stages though, with a two-nil victory in the bag, did their neat manipulation assume a negative air. One of those who shone amid this string-pulling composure was a certain Wim van Hanegem: even if his right boot may as well have been left at Feyenoord, or even in the shop with all his other right boots. Someone else who took the eye was their attacking right midfielder, a youngster still short of his nineteenth birthday, his promise bought early from Haarlem: Johnny Metgod, complete with a full head of hair. As for Twente, meanwhile, not even Frans Thijssen or substitute Arnold Mühren could make an impact, although their sweeper Epi Drost was impressive in restricting the scoreline. Eighteen years later Drost, at the age of only forty-nine, would be one of two former Twente players to die of heart attacks, whilst another – Jan Jeuring, who also turned out against AZ – survived one in 1994. A link was suggested when Dick Oosthoek, Twente's club doctor in the early seventies, confessed to having administered banned drugs to improve players' performances.

AZ finished that 1976–77 season in third place. Prior to this achievement, in fact just three days after the game in Enschede, I would see two of their players again, but in a rather different setting.

Sir Alf had taken a dim view of Holland's performance on their first ever visit to Wembley in January 1970, calling it negative. Others had seen it in another light, and I was one. In my report of that goalless match for the FA Year Book, I wrote: "....the Netherlands played some of the finest possession football seen at Wembley for a very long time ....England became increasingly frustrated ....they had no solution to the controlled football of the skilful Dutch who found positions and stroked the ball around with surprising ease ...." England, though a little short of full-strength that night – no Bobby Moore, whilst Ian Storey-Moore made his only appearance – were in their heyday; the Dutch were in the dawn of their first. By February 9th 1977, their next appearance in

London, perception of their game had changed dramatically because they'd earned the right, through both achievement and performance, to be viewed with awe. During the previous seven years, four successive European Cups had been held aloft and the world had rejoiced over their football in the 1974 World Cup, which only ironic disconcert in the Final itself – van Hanegem said half the team concentrated not on cementing their early lead but on merely wanting to humiliate the West Germans – surely prevented their winning.

Gut reactions risk flaw and often danger, but one of mine is that in thirty years of watching England the finest performance I've seen is that of Holland in 1977, and my head would probably follow my heart anyway. Is perfection possible on a football pitch? As near as damn it (no phonetic pun intended), yes. What I saw was certainly immaculate at least.

Ten outfield players utterly at ease anywhere on the pitch, all aware of each other and of their responsibilities. Playing with an edge but without fear. Keeping the ball so the opposition can't hurt you. Adroit under challenge. Making space, providing passing options. Precision. Technical excellence. Vision. Unpredictability, switching positions, mixing long passes with short, changing direction and the tempo. Prudence within a positive attitude of self-confident development. Defending impenetrably when without the ball. Making your command count by winning the match and keeping a clean sheet. Rendering your opponents wholly impotent and demoralised. Warming the hearts of the public.

What else is there to be done? Holland did it all this night. Their style was labelled, in a throwaway manner, "Total Football". Actually, it was virtually the realisation of the Austrian Willy Meisl's vision of the future expounded in his book *Soccer Revolution* twenty-two years earlier: football played in ever-fluid rotation by all-rounders and giving full rein to individual expression within collective responsibility. The Dutch, as they had for some time by now, came mighty close to Meisl's "Whirl". How absolutely delighted the old boy would have been.

Hugo Hovenkamp, AZ's left-back, made his international debut in this match, and Kees Kist, their centre-forward, came on for Johnny Rep ten minutes from the end. Whilst in 1970 all the Dutch players had been home-based, things were different now: Rep was at Valencia, Rensenbrink at Anderlecht, and Barcelona had Neeskens and the master-orchestrator Cruyff. With the richest forward talent leaving the country, Dutch league attendances were even less, and so were obstacles to the Molenaars' intent. Both of Holland's goals in that 2–0 triumph were scored by the hugely gifted midfielder Jan Peters of NEC Nijmegen. That summer, he was transferred as well. To AZ.

Peters was missing when I watched AZ's visit to Ajax in February 1980. Indeed, his knee injury caused him to miss many games that season, and the suspect joint had in fact made Ajax back out of signing him before AZ took the plunge.

Such was the interest in this match – Ajax were reigning Champions, while AZ had finished third again then fourth in the past two seasons and beaten Ajax in the 1978 Cup Final for their first ever trophy – that the fixture was taken to Amsterdam's Olympic Stadium. This seemed to me to underline AZ's arrival as a team to be reckoned with, especially as Ajax' average attendance at their modest De Meer ground had dipped to below ten thousand.

The venue was a relic indeed. Built for the 1928 Games – appropriately, given Amsterdam's liberal air, the first to admit women; and the last where football really mattered, since the inaugural World Cup was two years away – its predominantly brick setting, whilst hardly palatial by modern standards and bearing more than a hint of decay, certainly held a historical aura. Two significant physical features were its tall Marathon Tower, which the victorious Uruguayan footballers remembered when the Estadio Centenario went up in Montevideo, and its floodlights, Europe's first permanent structures back in 1934. As with all relics, though, such features best serve to evoke. This was where Eusébio had slugged it out with Puskás for the 1962 European Cup. More momentous had been a foggy night towards the end of 1966.

When nineteen-years-old Johan Cruyff and his Ajax cohorts glided out of the mist here in a European Cup-tie to demolish 5–1 Shankly's bewildered Liverpool of Yeats, St John, Hunt and the rest, they sent the capacity 60,000 crowd into delirium, but they also seemed, while heralding the birth of a major new force at club level, to be delivering Dutch football itself from the haze of an antiquated past into the modern age at last. Joining Ajax at the same time as another icon, coach Rinus Michels, Cruyff became only the club's second full-time professional, that structure not having been established in The Netherlands till as late as 1954. Despite having been a founder member of FIFA in 1904 and managing three Olympic bronzes in the early years of the century, the Dutch game had languished in a football backwater and not even professionalism had prevented the odd drowning, as in October 1963 when Luxembourg eliminated them from the European Nations' Cup. But those intoxicating Ajax sides as the sixties decade entered the next, and for all that arch-rivals Feyenoord got their hands on the premier trophy first, saw the mainstream joined with a vengeance, and provided the inspiration to keep sailing, not least because of their innovative nature. That fresh style, too, would be developed into a fine art for the national side by a freakish new generation of playing talent, and would be hugely instrumental in propelling football itself from its often brutally negative philosophy of the sixties. Holland's ship had transformed itself from a hulk into the world's leading ferry. That said, it had slowed down by this day and indeed the next few years would see Dutch football becalmed. Having been the mere width of a goalpost away from winning the 1978 World Cup, when Rensenbrink's shot at the end of normal time would have sunk Argentina – again, so very near – the Netherlands would fail after 1980 to qualify for any major tournament until 1988. The next generation of superstars was still to aft. On this February Sunday afternoon, learning his trade at a Haarlem club on the verge of relegation was a short-haired seventeen-year-old called Ruud Gullit. On Ajax' conveyor belt were another 17-year-old half-Surinamese, Frank Rijkaard, and a 15-year-old named Marco van Basten.

On their team sheet now was only one name to really conjure with, Ruud Krol, although the Danes Frank Arnesen and Soren Lerby would enjoy high-profile careers and goalkeeper Piet Schrijvers accumulated nearly fifty appearances for the Netherlands. As for AZ, apart from Peters and the now departed van Hanegem, their familiar names were present, under the direction of German coach George Kessler who'd been in charge of that Dutch national team which had irritated Ramsey ten years earlier. The Molenaars had appointed Kessler in the summer of 1978 and would never regret it.

There were: Ronald Spelbos, a hard but ball-playing centre-back who would soon, though already approaching twenty-six, win the first of twenty-one caps; the cool and erect Hovenkamp, who'd win ten more than that, amusingly referred to in the match programme as "De man met een plank in zijn rug" ("rug" meaning back); the long-serving Danish playmaker Kristen Nygaard; Peter Arntz, a perceptive midfielder full of intelligent running; Johnny Metgod, by now betraying the balding process and converted to sweeper, though operating in midfield here, later of Nottingham Forest via Real Madrid; and above all the curly blond Kist, sharp as a tack, scorer of 113 goals in four seasons from 1976–77 to 1979–80. A year later it was estimated that Kist's annual earnings were £120,000, as much as Rainer Bonhof at Cologne, much more than the Brazilian Falcao at Roma and Platini at St Etienne, and way more than the next highest paid in Holland, the van der Kerkhof twins at Philips-backed PSV Eindhoven, an indication of AZ's exceptional clout at a time when Dutch football was experiencing serious financial problems with all but a handful of clubs in debt.

The half-full stadium enjoyed a feast. Two evenly matched sides provided a particularly absorbing first half of a predictably pure brand, always movement off the ball and options. All the goals were scored prior to the break, too, resilient AZ recovering from a tenth-minute deficit when they left Lerby completely unmarked to wrest the lead within twelve minutes more. The "stiff-back" drilled home a 25-yarder and Kist, provider for once, measured a cross beyond Schrijvers for Metgod to head home. An incisive and very impressive midfielder called Dick Schoenaker levelled it after thirty-four minutes from a typically majestic, swerving ball by the inspirational Krol, soon of Napoli.

Schoenaker departed injured on the hour, just after AZ had hit the bar twice within moments, and the contest tailed off somewhat thereafter, although the closing ten minutes became end-to-end stuff as both sides strove for the spoils. Though Ajax had the edge territorially, it was fair that the spoils be shared. A measure of AZ's achievement was that until this afternoon Ajax had dropped only one point at home and had rattled in thirty-seven goals against just seven. In second place at kick-off, AZ thus remained five points adrift. The following season would climactically be different ....

It all seems sadly so long ago now. The Ajax supporters' club newspaper *De Ajacied* was advertising various scarves for sale, including those of eight top English teams. There were Liverpool, Manchester United, Arsenal, West Bromwich Albion ....

"Our football is more together!" I was told in a nearby bar by a group of Ajax fans. As if I didn't know.

I didn't see any trouble, either.

The first violent act I saw inside a Dutch football ground was so staggering that I wondered if I'd imagined it. I was at the Stadion Feyenoord, popularly known as 'De Kuip' (The Tub), Holland's largest, one of 50,000 present to watch a game against PSV Eindhoven in December 1975. The visitors had won the Championship the previous season, breaking a ten-year stranglehold of Ajax and Feyenoord, and were on their way to retaining it. The atmosphere and noise, so unusually for these trips of mine, were suitably charged. Feyenoord won 1–0 but the nature of their winning goal so enraged a PSV defender that he sprinted over to the linesman away to my left and really got in his face. After a few seconds' dialogue something happened that I've only ever seen once since, when our linesman wore jeans and his flag was a Safeway carrier bag on Billesley Common one Sunday morning. The PSV defender hit the turf. The linesman had nutted him. That was also the day, impressed by the brass wind support of the locals, that I bought a horn, intending to blow Albion towards promotion. "Your horn's an offensive weapon," said the police officer who confiscated it at Bootham Crescent.

It's generally believed that it was a match involving Feyenoord which gave rise to the organised hooliganism that began to afflict Dutch football in the mid-seventies. The excesses of Tottenham fans in Rotterdam when Spurs lost the 1974 UEFA Cup Final appear to have touched a chord within the less scrupulous element of those who would consume the English youth culture. Our music was one thing, but this was much more thrilling. Inevitably it would spread – through challenge – particularly to those young fans of other large city clubs: Den Haag, Utrecht, but especially Ajax. The cities of Rotterdam and Amsterdam have historically sought to out-perform the other, after all. The copycat theory is given weight by the self-labelling with which the agitators advertised themselves. In those days before English groups bestowed upon themselves more esoteric titles – which the Dutch never seem to have done: perhaps simply by choice, content to prolong the label – the Dutch purloined from English television the idea of an announceable 'end'. Thus Ajax' 'F-Side' and Feyenoord's 'Vak S', sectors of stadia where they congregated like the Park Lane or North Bank, became the battle-cries. The whole business developed and sustained such a foothold that by the start of the 1997–98 season entry to any Dutch ground in the top two divisions was dependent upon possession of a Club Card, a membership scheme designed as the latest measure to combat the plague. This wouldn't, however, stop five hundred Feyenoord fans, who travelled to Germany in January 1999 for a friendly fixture, from rampaging through the streets of Leverkusen. Nor would it prevent serious rioting three months later in central Rotterdam, when Feyenoord fans massed to celebrate their league championship triumph and Dutch police fired live bullets into them.

I once read a book on the subject of fan violence that included a chapter on the rise of the Dutch version. Psychologists, educationalists, anthropologists and sociologists wrote it, with the assistance of survey research centrists. All manner of scale coefficients and whatever were used in tabulated analysis. What claptrap! And how futile! The simple, absolute truth is that since human life began on earth and for as long as it remains, some young males simply enjoy fighting, and others are buzzed by being close to it. So far as this afflicts football, the problem subsides when organised fighting is looked upon as unfashionable.

Initially, in The Netherlands, I saw oafishness. At Ajax in April 1976, after a match against NAC Breda, with police conspicuous by their absence, I watched a few laughing home fans drop soft drink cans upon the departing visitors. It was a bit like children chucking snowballs. Ditties involved "la, la, la" – really, how threatening – pronounced, in that loud, guttural, northern Continental way, "lor, lor, lor". Silly. At Enschede, on the day I first admired AZ, where again I noticed no police or stewards inside the ground, I watched two boys aged about ten wander around for a full quarter of an hour collecting cans and hurling them as far as they could towards the pitch without reprimand (the cans landed no further than the perimeter track). After that match I saw a handful of teenagers mess with a train compartment. Silly.

But at Venlo, in March 1977, my perception changed. A mob of around a hundred and fifty Ajax fans congregated at one end of the strange little stadium valleyed into the earth. There was some fighting prior to kick-off, but it was at half-time that real viciousness erupted. Till then, yet again, the only security had taken the form of a few plain-clothed men patrolling the perimeter of the pitch with dogs. Now, though, the police arrived. The stadium was indeed peculiarly arranged. Terracing had been constructed in pens with huge chunks of rough earth in between, and around three sides stretched a wide walkway that formed this terracing into two stages. The walkway's width was sufficient to drive a police wagon along, and that's what happened: to see the flashing blue light amid the spectators' heads was weird! Having come to a halt at the scene, half a dozen officers burst out wielding truncheons, waded into the action, picked out the Ajax ringleaders, chucked them head-first over the wall, and helped colleagues stuff them into the wagon. Another wagon then arrived and stayed for the second half as a deterrent. The whole episode was as savage as any I'd ever seen.

If that was the F-Siders, I saw examples of Vak S' self-glorification at Vitesse Arnhem in October 1979, where some of their huge following – rowdy only on this day – now sported 'Fighting Squadron' scarves and 'The Best Fighters of The World' badges: yes, of course, in English.

They came together at De Kuip in January 1982 – Rijkaard and the returned Cruyff played for Ajax, van Hanegem again for Feyenoord, in a 2–2 draw watched by another throbbing 50,000 crowd – to provide a brawl for my interval entertainment. Some rivalries really do involve sheer hatred, given libertine vent and fed by the growth of organised so-called hooliganism, a hatred that in England has in cases survived the crept unfashionableness. And some Ajax and Feyenoord fans genuinely hated each other so much that many years after I'd last seen any of their kind over there, in March 1997, they actually staged a mass non-matchday showdown on wasteland that caused one of them, the F-Side leader, to die beneath iron bars.

That reality said, I still believe the Dutch manifestation was born of imitation. The England-Holland match at Wembley on the evening of 23rd March 1988 was played amid tight security measures, partly because of a perceived threat posed by Dutch troublemakers (who braved nothing), partly as an instructional exercise for the benefit of visiting West German police officials with Euro '88 around the corner. Aside from Holland's beautiful second goal, the climax of twenty passes, the other thing I chiefly remember is some chorus midway through the second half. It had nothing to do with the contest and nothing, really, to do with football. It smacked only of self-annunciation in the tone of false counter-challenge. "Utrecht! Utrecht!"

I've always had a sneaking suspicion that, amongst faddists, the incidence of masturbation is especially high. Perhaps there's a scale coefficient somewhere.

I felt sad when I last watched AZ at a full-house De Meer in October 1982. Their fine team had largely broken up, only Hovenkamp and Arntz remaining of those artists I'd so admired. This shadow played a stiff, graceless, negative 4-4-2 and could barely handle a free-spirited Ajax, whose goals came from the gifted Gerald Vanenburg and Jesper Olsen. Hovenkamp was substituted twenty-five minutes from the end; Arntz was later booked following an altercation with Lord Cruyff, and was visibly upset when the crowd subsequently booed his every touch of the ball.

Kessler's touch – assisted by Hans Eijkenbroek, his Dutch captain at Wembley back in 1970 – had by then delivered to the club its wonderful success, though. Only once since 1964 has a side other than Ajax, Feyenoord or PSV won the Dutch Championship: that side was AZ in 1981, and they did so by a runaway twelve-point margin, sealing the title with a 5-1 thumping of Feyenoord in Rotterdam. Not only that, they comfortably beat Ajax 3-1 in the Cup Final that year for the pinnacle of a tremendous double. The Cup was also won the following year. In 1981, too, they reached the UEFA Cup Final, where although an uncharacteristically cautious display incurred a 0-3 defeat at Bobby Robson's Ipswich, AZ were sweet – if in vain – during a 4-2 second-leg victory in the Olympic Stadium.

But after 1982's Cup triumph and another third placing in the league, the fairytale would indeed be no more. A return to mediocrity stretched to an even worse fate in 1988, when with ironic timing – just as triumphs by PSV in the European Cup and the national side in the European Championships in that same year heralded the Netherlands' return to glory – AZ were relegated. They were unfortunate, too: their twenty-eight points from thirty-four games would normally have earned comfort, while a last-day fixture between PEC Zwolle and Volendam produced a goalless draw that ensured safety for both but invited allegations of match-fixing. Eight years in the wilderness, with attendances dipping close to three thousand, ended in 1996 – but re-acquaintance with the top flight brought only instant relegation again. Then, this time as coach, van Hanegem came back: and so did AZ in 1998.

So, too, did I this March 1999, revisiting their stadium for the first time in twenty-one years. Alkmaar itself, dating back to AD800 as a settlement amid sand dunes and lagoons, and growing up around the huge, limestone St Laurens Church, had expanded even more with its urban and industrial development of the 1970s, so that its population today nudged a hundred thousand. It's a clean environment, though. Three-quarters of the workforce are engaged in the services sector, and the town itself provides a lovely example of unhurried, harmless, litter-free, provincial Holland. Its waterways are prominent, its alleyways shop-cluttered, its old quarter around the Waagplein the nicest, most characterful spot: elaborately gabled terraces linked by hump-backed canal bridges, and fairy-lit after dark as the Amstel goes down. The route I retraced carried me past the smart residences of long, wide Westerweg before a left turn into Prinses Julianalaan deposited me in thick woodland. Through the treetops, past a small park with duckpond where dutiful daughters wheeled aged mothers, close to a church spire, I spied a floodlight pole or two. I was back at the home of something that once upon a time had put the town on the map for other than its centuries-old, tourist-trap cheese market, and had provided sport other than the dodging of criss-crossing cyclists.

Like so many Dutch stadia, greenery to the fore, AZ's training pitches lay behind the main stand, and I was just in time to see the winding down of a session, a game of two-touch. Then someone with dark curly hair and thick eyebrows tidied up by sending the loose balls towards a gatherer. This he did not with his right foot. From thirty yards, five plopped into the held sack without its being moved an inch. The sixth chip was a few inches off target. Van Hanegem and the other tracksuit were laughing.

I discovered that Henk van Rijnsoever, a defender in that team of old, was now the club's commercial manager; Peter Arntz was commercial assistant; Hugo Hovenkamp was on the training staff. It was warming to see such links with the past. The orderly stadium, too, seemed instantly recognisable, even though it was now wholly covered and had sprouted red seats on three sides, so reducing its capacity to just over eleven thousand (back in those late seventies, 20,900 had flocked here for a visit by Ajax). Somehow, it remained indeed emblematic of the club. Whereas several Dutch outfits now enjoyed spanking new grounds – not only had Ajax moved into the futuristic Amsterdam Arena and 'De Kuip' been given a major facelift with a roof, but even Vitesse Arnhem's Gelredome was sheer space-age – this was a homely place, neat and very pleasing to the eye. Contrarily, though, its modesty seemed an inappropriate stage for that handful of players who'd been genuinely of world class.

Sitting in the deserted hush this Thursday noon, I looked to my left above its terraced side – the Molenaar Tribune – and shared the memory with the still, tall trees. This was where Metgod, Peters, van Hanegem, Kist and the rest had outclassed Den Haag. I smiled in recalling that two of Den Haag's players, Martin Jol and Romeo Zondervan, had subsequently joined my own team. When I looked towards the main stand on my right I saw exactly where I'd sat that afternoon and, quite startlingly, now remembered a tiny ramp in front of the seating. At that time it had seemed strangely unnecessary, a little concrete dash of design; right now it became a focus for what time on earth had brought since.

What that brought to AZ today, upliftingly, was consolidation back in the top division. Despite having been recently slaughtered 2–8(!) at Roda JC, the team was sitting snugly in mid-table, having lost just four of its twenty-three league games. I hoped the club was here to stay, to grow again. Of all my 'other teams', AZ is my favourite.

By the fervid evening of Tuesday 18th June 1996, yet another generation of Dutch master-footballers – if, typically by now, prone to ego-driven factionalism – had come to the fore. A young Ajax side had scintillatingly won the previous year's European Cup and those players, augmented by the likes of Bergkamp, formed the majority of the Netherlands team that faced England in the European Championships. Terry Venables – how I wish he'd stayed in charge – said it was "the most satisfying night ever for me". Whilst our 4–1 triumph avenged humiliation at Euro '88 and our failure at the hands of the Dutch to qualify for USA '94, his satisfaction was born of more positive stuff. An ardent admirer of Holland, and Ajax in particular, Venables had studied at great length how to overcome them, so there was tremendous pride in demoralising them and hearing their coach, Hiddink, admit that England had been wholly superior. "Close to perfection," was Venables' verdict upon the performance. The whole nation shared his delight; and some of us recalled a Wembley night in February 1977.

Sometimes, now, should I flick through old copies of *Voetbal International* and perhaps catch photographs of a fresh-faced Ronald Koeman of Groningen or a slim Louis van Gaal of Sparta Rotterdam, the memories flood back. Lovely land, lovely football.

Chapter 6
Into the Honi Trap

East Germany: Carl Zeiss Jena v WBA 19/9/79

Jimmy met us on the platform and took us to the waiting bus. Portly and be-spectacled, he was aged around fifty-five. His face seemed that of a man who had once known decency and neighbourliness, but its attempts at joviality over the next couple of days seemed from distant memory. Jimmy wasn't his real name. When he introduced himself as our guide, he didn't give it, and no-one asked. He wasn't really a guide, either. Although he knew our little nickname for him, we never knew the codename for the little operation that saw him cast as watchdog.

September 1979 belonged to an age that appears unrepeatable in more ways than one. Germany was split into two, and West Bromwich Albion had a team to be seriously reckoned with. The previous season had seen us finish third in the Championship and reach the quarter-finals of the UEFA Cup, and now we were engaged in the latter competition again. The ideal draw for any fan want-ing to follow his team abroad, of course, is a side who not only come from an attractive part of the Continent but also against whom you fancy your chances. A less than formidable outfit from perhaps Spain or Greece would be nice. So our destination as we eased out of Birmingham's New Street Station one mild Saturday evening provided nothing of the kind: the town of Jena, which lay mysteriously the other side of the Iron Curtain in East Germany. Very few Albion fans would make this trip – but our own, independent party trusting the train numbered no less than twelve. The expedition had been meritoriously ar-ranged by a remarkable sixteen-stone character from Tamworth called Ray, who'd fixed up the hotel accommodation prior to our setting out, a necessary measure to satisfy conditions of entry into this grim bastion of totalitarianism.

Ray's organisational prowess as the erstwhile secretary of the Tamworth branch of the Albion Supporters' Club had been best illustrated up in Newcas-tle a couple of years earlier. As we'd stood outside a city-centre chip shop at half-past five we'd seen his lonesome bulk loom on the horizon and descend panting, beer belly wobbling, towards us at the most frantic pace he could muster, to utter the immortal words, "Ay! 'Ave y'seen our bleedin' coach?"

On other occasions he'd displayed a ruinous tendency to get the departure times of last trains round his chopper, too, despite his actually being employed by British Rail. Thus we'd been required to hitch-hike home from Preston, at one point being attacked by a pack of Jack Russell terriers along Watling Street in the dark small hours, and to negotiate an urgent beeline over the tracks from the wrong platform at Oporto Station to grab the Paris train by the skin of our teeth. So his fixing of this trip had thrown back a few sniggers.

His more customary colours came to the fore, however, after we'd disembarked at Ostend. Hunger filled the cold night air. "Ah know a brilliant place," enthused Colonel Ray. "Follow me!" Dutifully, we did. Ten minutes later, by when his confident march at the head of the column had assumed a more tentative step, he assured us that he now definitely had his bearings and a succulent chicken for all lay just around the next corner. It didn't. "Fuck me, Ray," said long-haired, big-nosed Mick. "Eh?" said Ray, a stupefied gawp on his fat features. We stood there, the dozen of us, bags on the grubby cobbled street, and every deserted avenue on the compass looked exactly the same.

Eventually we did rediscover the still lively quarter but before long had incurred the plaintive wrath of a small young chap who worked as a carpenter with Mick, and was known affectionately, for obvious reasons, as Lardhead. At the passport control some two hours earlier, as he took it upon himself to lead our invasion of Europe, he'd greeted the Belgian official's enquiry as to where we were travelling with a flummoxed turnaround and an agitated cry of, "Mick! Where'm we gooin'?"

This had indeed been a genuine question, and given that even Sir Matt Busby could never pronounce Benfica correctly, it could hardly be expected of Lardhead to deliver on request such a mouthful as Carl Zeiss Jena. The official, though, sat unimpressed and since he refused to accept that anyone could be so thick as to not know where he was heading, he presumed sarcasm. "We also ken be awkward, you may find," had been his stern warning as he slapped Lardhead's passport back into his hand. Now, as we left one bar, music still blaring, Lardhead caught up with us in the street. "Dunna bother t'tell me when y'goo, will yuh?" Coincidentally he'd just resurfaced after catching up on some shut-eye in the deepest, darkest recess of another bar opposite, which the rest of us had already vacated half an hour earlier, unbeknown to Lardhead who assumed we'd just that minute forsaken him. The Colonel wasn't so lucky. Mick and myself eventually stumbled upon De Koekoek, enjoyed some succulent chicken and thick brown bread, and told Ray all about it afterwards.

We took the opportunity of watching a couple of games this day. During the morning we happened upon a junior game which had attracted a couple of hundred spectators to the park where it was being played, so it must have been a pretty important affair to some. The kids looked to be of the twelve to thirteen age group, although the standard had more in common with a junior school's games period. Towards the end Mick decided a substitution was the order of the day, and after nipping beneath the surrounding rope he began to limber up along the touchline, past the managers' benches, occasionally bursting into a sprint. Quite the opposite of being ushered away, his self-delegated role of reserve-de-luxe was greeted with amused intrigue, especially when he trotted to a halt beside the bench, proceeded to lean forward and then, holding each ankle in turn, began flexing his legs in a pose that lay somewhere between David Fairclough and a deranged ballet dancer. Despite not being called into the fray, he at least retired from the scene to a round of applause. This was also afforded him a few hours later in the quaint setting of A.S. Oostende's tiny stadium, where two thousand had turned out to watch the home side play Herentals in a third division match. It was dross. We were planted behind a goal, and just in front were a group of oafish home supporters waving their red and green flags with all the relevance of a track marshal after the last racing car has gone home. "Ah-Es-Oh! Ah-Es-Oh!" they chanted rapidly in homage. "Arse-Oles!" cried Mick, whereupon some buffoon turned round and misguidedly clapped this participation of the new English branch of the A.S.O. Supporters' Club, several members of which were prostrate on the terracing with their eyes closed and making noises in accordance with the colourfully named match programme, *Rood Groen.*

Our party split into several groups that night – our second without seeing a bed – having arranged to rendezvous early the next morning for the ride into West Germany. Towards midnight, four of us found ourselves in a knocking-shop. While Ray flopped himself down at a table to contemplate the remainder of the route, possibly involving connections from Zurich, I perched on a bar stool, beleaguered by a lady of the night. Hamburg's Reeperbahn, Amsterdam, Antwerp, wherever, it's always the same. Some resident tart sidles next to you, smilingly opens the conversation by asking where you're from and how long you're staying, soon places a hand titillatingly upon your person, and eventually asks you to buy her a drink, which is always some cocktail costing a bomb. Should your cock want to come away with a tale to tell, the bomb becomes nuclear. She was attractive, blonde, late-twenties like myself, although her appeal was dented by the discoloured state of her teeth, a dull yellow. Three bodies away to my left sat Mick. Immediately to his right was a hag. The hag's right hand was inside the jumper of a fetishist beanpole from Tividale who was known to his friends as Lionel Lamp-post. I tried to listen in to their conversation, despite a left hand inching ever closer to my groceries. Lionel was remaining deadpan. "You have seece children?" ejaculated the old boot. "My – what a man!" Her hand massaged his back admiringly. "But I cannot believe!" "S'roight," chipped in Mick. "An' fower of 'em's black!"

The music aborted, the carrots undangled, frowns abounding, we staggered onward. The sight that greeted us in the next bar, a greasers' hang-out, was that of someone slumped hunched against a wall, asleep despite Thin Lizzy, as grinning leather-garbed locals saw how many ashtrays they could stack on his head, actively encouraged by familiar faces. Eventually the pile numbered eight before he stirred and shot up like a startled pigeon, awakened by the sound of crashing tin. Pained by this, he asked me to take him to the beach so he could get a few hours' undisturbed sleep. The temperature outside at this hour, at a guess, was not far off freezing. Lardhead.

After a journey lasting four hours, taking us through Brussels, Liège and Aachen, we arrived at Cologne, the busiest railway station in West Germany with more than a hundred international connections and, all told, over nine hundred trains a day crossing the Hohenzollern Bridge approach. One of Germany's oldest cities, founded by the Romans in Julius Caesar's day, it had been virtually flattened during the Second World War, but now formed a prime illustration of the Federal Republic's urban renewal and economic recovery. Amid its smart modern buildings and pedestrianised precincts, however, there were still many instances of lovingly restored architecture dating back centuries, whilst several museums celebrated Cologne's historical, commercial and cultural significance. The city's appeal, of course, was heightened by the majestic presence of the Rhine, the main artery of Western Europe, and many a boat trip embarked here for a picturesque cruise.

A handful of us resolved to climb the five hundred and nine steps up Cologne's most celebrated landmark, the twin-spired cathedral, Europe's tallest building until Eiffel pricked the heavens above Paris. Ray's companion in rueful distress was Denis, a fellow fatty from Tipton, barely used to walking never mind mountaineering. Generous of disposition too, Denis over the years had confounded all and sundry by his faultless night driving from some far-flung away game despite his having consumed as much ale as everyone else, when attempts at assisting him with navigation would quickly degenerate into mere snoring. We were all rewarded with an incredible panoramic view, stretching even as far as the tranquil Siebengebirge, the Seven Hills beyond Bonn, as the Rhine meanwhile became a silver ribbon.

A few Kölsch beers found their way down prior to our heads hitting most welcome pillows, and during the course of that session I sensed that Cologne possessed a more fun-loving outlook than other places I'd visited in West Germany. It wasn't exactly Munich during Oktoberfest, but a bar crawl around the Altstadt area was a joyous experience, despite one offering of toilet graffiti that boasted "Nottingham Lads Took Cologne" – a relic of Forest's European Cup victory here the previous season. Forest, through a last-match streaky win at The Hawthorns back in May, had squeezed us from the runners-up spot, which made me hate them all the more. Anyway, beneath this typically graceless, somewhat sad, wall-marking, someone else had inscribed "So What? I Bought It!"

Nobody in his right mind, though, would have wanted to possess that place we'd be seeking the next day.

We all made it to the station in good time for the early half-hour ride to Düsseldorf, where we'd have to change for the long final leg of our haul. Even at this hour, when most folk's alarm clocks back home would only just be blowing off, the waiting area was crowded. Lionel, possibly dreaming of ringing Anita Ward's bell, had succumbed to the lingering desire for further kip, and as usual when in such a state, his mouth while he lolled back in his seat formed a gaping pit as if awaiting the dentist's drill. Instead, it received a liberal dose of salt from the table, administered by Denis. The Boche found this hilarious, but I feared The Lamp would now be pestering me for one of the cans I'd saved for the journey, and so he did. This left me with just the one, which I could no longer resist shortly after leaving Düsseldorf, and I sat on a corridor seat to drink it in peace. Unfortunately, as I put it down for a moment while gazing out of the window, a ticket inspector came along and kicked the damned thing over, and although he must have been aware of what he'd done, rather maddeningly didn't apologise. "Wer hat der Krieg gewonnen?" I called after him with a patriotic phrase I remembered from schooldays. He halted: then carried on regardless. Well, who did win the bloody war?

Certainly not the poor folk imprisoned in East Germany. We reached the border point at Gerstungen at around half-past three that afternoon. Onto the train strode the uniforms with their guns, and after examining our documents and stamping our passports, they asked how much of their currency we were bringing in – knowing full well that it was prohibited to do so. This seemed immediately to set the tone of suspicion that would prevail towards us throughout our stay.

And then we were behind the Curtain. With a mixture of awe and repugnance, we viewed the fence winding its deathly way towards the horizon, its forbiddingness emphasised at regular intervals by those grim watchtowers guarding the inviolability of this Marxist paradise. Propaganda had it that the purpose of the minefields and automatic guns was to keep out foreign provocateurs. The whole world knew that they were there to trap people inside, such a heaven on earth that those who attempted escape were shot without qualm.

Leaving the frontier behind, the train would labour on for a further two hours before reaching Jena, a distance of around seventy miles. The most remarkable feature of the journey was the scarcity of cars, whilst the few that did appear along the countryside roads looked at first glance reminiscent of those seen back home a quarter of a century before. These were Trabants, in theory the German Democratic Republic's equivalent of the Volkswagen, in reality a spluttering little freak built of plastic with a two-stroke engine that folk, on average, waited nine years to collect. Quite startlingly, this lack of modernity also applied to buses, their bonnets heavily pregnant, and the whole experience indeed seemed like a dream set back in time, an impression illustrated all the more by the sight of men and women working their collective farms by hand, not a machine in sight.

Through Eisenach (birthplace of Johann Sebastian Bach) and Gotha, past Erfurt (where Martin Luther attended university) and Weimar (the first meeting place of Germany's national assembly after World War One, and where the

UEFA-Cup-
Wettbewerb 1979/80
1. Runde

Mittwoch
Ernst-Abbe-
Sportfeld

19. 9.
1979

17.00
Uhr

West Bromwich Albion

Nr. 4/1979/80

Programmheft 0,30 M

new republican constitution was famously drafted) – and we finally arrived at our destination a few minutes after six o'clock.

Upon collection we were ferried, amid curious stares, to the teasingly-named Hotel International for our two-night stay. Its brochure boasted an "excellent cuisine", but after a none too palatable dinner in its rather drab restaurant, despite a six-piece band in traditional costume trying to project a convivial atmosphere, we left Jimmy's gaze and ventured out to explore.

Jena, with a population of a hundred thousand, was situated in the south of the GDR within the lushly forested region of Thuringia, together with the Baltic coast a favourite spot for holidaying East Germans. Fifty miles away lay Czechoslovakia. Forty miles away stood Bavaria. Our arrival in this area coincided with a mind-blowing escape to the latter just two days earlier. Sixteen miles south of Jena lay the village of Pössneck, and from a nearby field under the cover of darkness in the cold early hours of Sunday morning two young families had fled to the West. The means of their miraculous escape was a home-made hot air balloon, stitched from nylon sheets and curtains, and with a tiny wooden raft secured only by a clothes line. Of all the ingenious methods of fleeing East Germany – one man had built a micro-submarine using a cycle motor to cross the Baltic to Denmark – this was surely the most spectacular. They'd been lucky: searchlights had sought them, but the contraption had managed to rise above the beams, whilst on their eventual bump to earth they hadn't been certain that they'd gone far enough. Years later I would view this craft in a museum near the old Checkpoint Charlie, and be totally flabbergasted by its flimsiness. The youngest of the four children involved was only two years old, testimony indeed to their desperation. As the man who designed the balloon, Peter Strelzyk, said, "...it was no longer possible for us to lie to our children and put up with the political conditions..."

Political conditions in Jena were nevertheless being glorified right now, since several buildings were festooned with huge red flags bearing the Soviet hammer and sickle, while other red drapes proclaimed "30 Jahre". This was all in celebration of the fact that it was now thirty years since the political division of Germany:this saw the three occupation zones of the Western Allies, following World War Two, become reunited into a Federal State that would enter NATO, while the Russians retained their sector in eastern Germany and drew it into the Communist Warsaw Pact. Thirty years of dogma; thirty years of suppression; thirty years of deceit. Anyone exalting the doctrine of Communism from their faraway cushy sofa in 1979 should have visited East Germany with an open mind and then have been thankful that they could go home the same way. They would have discovered that instead of being a process of liberation, in reality it was the opposite, repressing body and heart. The party was omnipotent in the name of the people, but it was the people's worst enemy because it murdered initiative. It was also omnipresent – a power based on fear. Perhaps the most frightening aspect was that new generations were growing up none the wiser, their mentalities imbued from birth: witness Herr Strelzyk's words regarding his kids.

Jena in a free society might have been considered quite a charming location as far as its surroundings were concerned. Situated in the Saale River valley, the skyline offered pleasantly rolling, wooded hills, and a panorama as seen from Landgraf Hill showed that much of the town itself was consumed by greenery. Not so very far away lay the Harz Mountains where the Grimm brothers dreamed a fairy tale or two. Thuringia, indeed, had bred or inspired several luminaries, not just Luther and the Bach family. Goethe, author of *Faust*, spent five years in Jena around the turn of the nineteenth century; his friend Schiller, author of *William Tell*, spent ten; and the Hungarian-born composer Franz Liszt, father-in-law of Wagner, had strong connections with Weimar, as did Nietzsche. How ironic it all seemed that such spirit enrichment should have sprung from a cradle that was now tethered behind barbed wire. That said, six miles north of Weimar had been Buchenwald.

Unlike many places in the Eastern bloc, for example Magdeburg and even Prague, Jena had been spared too many of those grimly uniform, high-rise flats so emblematic of the totalitarian authorities. One monstrosity, nevertheless, loomed all of four hundred feet tall, a contrasting stone's throw from the fourteenth-century town hall with its baroque tower guarding the market square: resembling Birmingham's Rotunda, but even more grisly, this phallus had been erected only recently and been presented to Jena's 400-year-old university. It looked utterly incongruous amid the town's otherwise ageing architecture, sometimes medieval, and often decaying. Such was the extent of this peeling away that any quaintness yielded to ugliness. And the society being what it was, the overbearing atmosphere of dispirited subdual with which Jena was smitten suffocated any consideration of physical environment.

As we roamed the streets on this Tuesday night, we found them largely and eerily deserted. I saw only one cinema, and bars assumed the nature of oases. The couple we entered were stark, canteen-like, their few faces wary of our intrusion. Resigned faces too, lacking spontaneity or dynamism. No laughter. No singing. Definitely no jukeboxes. No gangs of kids out to enjoy themselves. Jesus, what did the young do here?

Thirty glorious years under the Reds or not, any celebration was decidedly lost upon one character we encountered. He was none other than a young off-duty soldier whom we'd stopped to ask where else we could find a drink, and he obligingly escorted us to one bar where he soon revealed his reason for such compliance. His name was Andreas and not to put too fine a point on it, he was thoroughly pissed off. He was also in the process of getting pissed, and while we – Mick, Denis, Ray and myself – silently questioned his prudence, he let it be known that he didn't give a damn. He seized this opportunity of telling us how he detested the army life, how he detested his existence. He really poured out his hatred to us, and he quite endeared himself because of this devil-may-care attitude. I looked around for any interested eavesdroppers. Any reporting was being compiled mentally in the bottom half of a beer glass. Eventually Andreas's head slumped onto the table, and we left. The barman was waiting to close. It was eleven o'clock. This wasn't Cologne. Outside again, one or two people were trickling out onto the streets. It looked like Jena itself was closing. We did find another bar, secluded, that was actually in full swing, with music and dancing. We weren't allowed in: a private do. And that was that – back to the hotel. Give me the degradation of the West any time.

The hotel offered a "dance bar", but as the dance floor was only slightly larger than a postage stamp and our group formed a two-thirds majority of the all-male clientele, Mick and I elected to retire. Looking down upon the deserted little square opposite, I sat on the window-sill of room 206, lit a cigarette, and cast an eye over the silent night scene. Away to the left shone a blue light. This was the Zeiss factory that dominated the town and, in 1966, had taken the local football club under its umbrella. Beginning in the mid-nineteenth century with only a small workshop from where he supplied spectacles to the townspeople, Carl Zeiss laid the foundations for a company that now boasted a worldwide reputation for its optical precision instruments: microscopes (Zeiss and the physicist Ernst Abbe together developed the first scientific model), binoculars, surveying and photographic equipment, astronomical and medical implements. Jena, with a population of just 6,000 when Carl Zeiss started out, had grown around this parent company which now possessed a total workforce of 45,000 people.

And, by Christ, Jena's working day began early! It was the sound of trams rattling past beneath the window that woke me, and when I got up to look outside the streets were teeming. It was 5 a.m.! Jimmy had already finished his breakfast by the time Mick and I eventually surfaced, and he announced that this morning we'd all be given a guided tour of the town, including a visit to its planetarium. Our guide would be someone else, he said, but he himself would meet us again for lunch before escorting us to the match.

The other guide was a tall, bearded fellow in his early forties, an intellectual type from the local university, and once again a very melancholy person. Whilst we formed the impression that Jimmy sometimes quite enjoyed forgetting himself in our company, this chap seemed somewhat awkward in his task. What they shared, though, was noticeable in their quiet moments, in their eyes. Whenever Jimmy removed his spectacles and thought we weren't looking, those faded eyes he rubbed would betray a defeat of the soul.

With a good command of our language, despite an embarrassing stutter, we were told now in no uncertain terms that "it is impossible to go round the factory": making us wonder to what other uses some of its products were put. However, we were taken round the shops, where the total absence of commercialism was almost untrue. One store, a small-scale equivalent of our supermarkets, was selling its food and household items in a manner utterly bereft of colour – no attractive signs shouting "fantastic offer" or "super saver", no eye-catching display, no seductive appeal. Just things laid out in bare, sober fashion, like some quartermaster's provisions. Were we supposed to be impressed? There was bound to be a reaction to this yawn-inducing exercise, where the stony faces of the locals were met by our blank ones. I watched Mick place a screwdriver off the shelf into someone's basket unnoticed, and again as he dropped a lump of cheese into another. Well, he was good for business. Further up the street, a sports outfitter's told a similar tale – absolutely no kit bore endorsement by a sporting personality. Definitely no deals here for Borg or Keegan. A little while later I stopped to buy a picture postcard of the town. They were all in black and white.

The Zeiss-Planetarium – the world's first public one – hosted a party of schoolchildren who gave us the usual inquisitive gawp as we were all ushered and hushed into our seats. Their notebooks and pencils offered a studious contrast to Lardhead, a frustrated looking Lionel, and the rest, who paid the bilingual commentator the courteous compliment of folding their arms and closing their eyes: even to the point of such total indifference whereby one of our group, a middle-aged chap named Bill Bithell, otherwise known as Bill Brothel, actually began snoring. Ray considerately gave him a nudge, whereupon he awoke with a resounding snort. This attempt by Ray to preserve decorum regrettably met with abject failure, however, for as the superimposed arrow flitted around on its solar teach-in, the resurrected Bill was soon heard by all and sundry to shout out, "Look! Thier's Concorde!" Amid the resulting cackles, I glanced through the dimness at our guide and saw a clear wince, as he continued to pick his nose. I hoped that the cause of his pain was not Bill's outburst but some over-ambitious harvesting.

Everyone appeared relieved at getting back outside and then, after accompanying us to a café not far from the hotel, this escort bade us farewell to resume his lectures. Before returning for lunch, which we had to do since Jimmy held our match tickets, we now had an hour to ourselves. Ale time. The previous evening had felt rather humid, and it was another bright but muggy day again, so thankfully we were able to drink in the open air by the market square. The beer was warm too, unfortunately, although we stomached three or four of them.

Back at the hotel there were some new arrivals. Besides the tiny official supporters' trip, a young Polish kid had travelled three hundred miles to give Albion his support. Apparently he'd followed our fortunes ever since the FA Cup triumph of 1968, and over the years had maintained contact with pen-pals and the club itself, particularly its shop – right now he was proudly sporting a blue and white striped shirt. There were also three Manchester City fans lending their presence on the way back from Warsaw where City had just played a friendly match with Legia, the former club of their major new signing, Polish national captain Kazimierz Deyna. This was pretty ironic since only the previous Saturday, prior to setting out, we'd all watched Albion defeat City 4–0. During the summer we'd bought a couple of players from Maine Road, England winger Peter Barnes and midfielder Gary Owen as replacements for the departed Laurie Cunningham (to Real Madrid, no less) and Len Cantello. Owen had been a particular favourite with City's supporters. "We thought we'd stop off 'ere an' 'ave a look at Gary," explained one. Jimmy's face almost ignited when they said they only had transit visas. They'd also changed their currency prior to leaving England, and instead of four East German marks to the pound as we'd been given here, they'd got seventeen. "No problems at the border?" I asked. "I stuck mine down me underpants," came a reply.

It had been a faltering start to the season by Albion. Losing the sorcerous Cunningham had been a major blow because more than any other player he'd embodied the excellence of the previous season. With his departure went much of our dynamic quality and irresistibility, most evident in thumping five goals at Old Trafford and dumping the Valencia of Kempes and Bonhof out of Europe. Another severe handicap had been the cartilage operation suffered by Cyrille Regis on the eve of the campaign, rendering him unavailable for some while yet, and with Owen and Barnes needing time to settle in, our freewheeling soul had disappeared and we were but a pale, stiff shadow. That Manchester City win had indeed been our first league victory and after six matches we were lying dismally at the wrong end of the table. As if to rub salt into our wounds, Barnes was out of this Jena match through injury too.

As for Jena themselves, we anticipated their being a tough nut to crack. Formed in 1946, they'd adopted their current name twenty years later when a minor revolution occurred in East German football. Initially – its FA had joined FIFA in 1952, after Germany itself had been thrown out immediately after the war – the national side had stood on the fringe of the international arena due to the political situation, merely playing friendlies against their Communist neighbours. It wasn't until the late 1950s that this arena had been tentatively joined: the qualifying competition for the 1958 World Cup was entered, as eventually were the three major European club competitions. Little headway had been made at any level, though, due not only to a shortage of talent but also to deficiencies in preparation. Sport being what it was to the Communist bloc's master politicians, a vehicle for raising the global profile of a successful State, and thus fostering pride among the populace – and East Germany being what it was to the Russian Bear, an embryo model with which to boast the triumph of its influence – corrective measures needed to be taken. In theory, of course, all Communist sportsmen were amateurs; but no country in the West in backing its sportsmen matched the State support system that came to exist behind the Iron Curtain. This extensive support – providing training facilities, coaching and funding – became channelled through certain outlets. So it was that in 1966 – around the time also that the fuse was being prepared for the imminent Olympics explosion of East Germany's athletes, heavily backed by Soviet aid – the masters decided that all football sections would be specially separated from existing multi-sports clubs and in many cases be placed in the charge of large industrial companies or State institutions, which provided good fronts. Thus did Motor Jena become Carl Zeiss Jena, better equipped to face the trials of that most prestigious of sports, football.

And they hadn't done badly, either. Domestically, due in no small way to a new scientific approach to training based upon co-operation with the university, they became such a formidable force in the late sixties and early seventies – going five years without a home defeat – that they came to form the bedrock of the national side. Their team manager Georg Buschner also took charge of the latter in April 1970, and within seven months had steered it to an entertaining performance at Wembley, where although a powerful England won 3–1, the East Germans had played a full part in providing a fine spectacle. No less than seven Jena players had been on duty that night, and the club would also be heavily represented in the team that Buschner took to the 1974 World Cup Finals where they famously defeated Beckenbauer and company, the eventual Champions, 1–0 in Hamburg. A historic night indeed, even though the smiles it drew in Moscow were probably more smug than those in Jena. Whilst it never attained the spectacular success achieved in the athletics stadium, swimming pool or other arenas, East German football had now commanded respect.

Jena had been quarter-finalists for each of the European competitions, in which they'd played fifty-eight matches, losing at home only three times. Their current team was a mixture of youth and experience – vastly so in the cases of two defenders, Kurbjuweit and the captain Weise, who'd played in Hamburg and by now had over a hundred and forty caps between them. Also still in the side, despite his thirty-six years, was left-winger Eberhard Vogel, scorer at Wembley.

Very fit, very well organised, and physically strong. But amateur? Weise and Kurbjuweit, indeed, had collected Olympic gold medals in Montreal three years earlier as East Germany won the football competition. How, then, were they and a few more Jena players taking home in excess of five hundred pounds a month, a small fortune? Because technically the Jena staff were all employees of the Carl Zeiss company. As George Orwell said, some people are more equal than others.

Jimmy led our group to the neat but small Ernst-Abbe-Sportfeld, enveloped thickly by trees and set against a backcloth of the picturesque Kernberg Peak. Save for a few seats beneath one small roof, the stadium was given entirely to open terracing, enough for 25,000, and it was two-thirds full. We were herded into a cordoned-off area at one corner, and stood there feeling rather like tolerated prisoners escorted outside for the day to some rehabilitative function. Two Germans – not Jimmy – stood with us. I subsequently saw a photograph of another tiny cluster of Albion fans in the seats. These included the Polish youth, Ryszard Fiszer. The photograph showed four unknown men in dark leather jackets, one of whom is staring fixedly into the lens. He would doubtless have spent much of the match looking fixedly at Fiszer, suspicious of his brazen support for the West. If these six men weren't Stasi then the Berlin Wall was an adventure playground. Over the lifespan of the GDR, the Stasi at its busiest possessed 97,000 full-time officers and 175,000 informers betraying colleagues, friends and even families, all in the name of State security. The population was told what to think, and if one of them belched at a portrait of Erich Honecker, the party head, they would have become one of six million files.

Hunting horns bellowed across the pitch from the sea of blue, yellow and white flags opposite, then the teams filed out, Jena in all-white, Albion looking decadent in green and yellow stripes, and Weise and John Wile each carried a bunch of red flowers. Mick was in non-subversive mood.

It was the very last match of our first hundred years' existence, and we were shit. "One of the worst performances I've seen from any team I've managed," fumed Ron Atkinson. Jena were powerful, urgent, dominant. Albion were anaemic. Jena's steamrollering produced two goals – no more, thankfully – and their nature was emblematic: a twenty-yard thunderbolt in the first half, and a thirty-yard rocket in the second. Also emblematic was our spurning a gilt-edged chance of a redeeming away goal in the very last minute. A low ball across the face of Jena's posts found David Mills totally unmarked. Mills had cost us a British record transfer fee (those were the days) of over half a million pounds nine months earlier. He put the ball over the bar. From having at last a truly exceptional team and genuine hopes of a glorious era of achievement, everything had gone wrong since May. That era never happened. Cunningham would eventually be followed out by Bryan Robson, taken to Old Trafford by Atkinson. The only real surprise as a football fan is if your dreams materialise.

Jena's fans didn't celebrate in the streets, which were virtually empty again that night. A curious feature, too, was the absence of police: but then according to Jimmy political crime was their chief concern. We couldn't have found any urge for vandalism, anyway. We were as downtrodden as everyone else by now. Lionel was vowing to flog his season ticket when he got back home to Tividale.

When we'd arrived, we'd been instructed to change a minimum of twenty pounds into their money. I still had over forty marks left at half-eleven and bugger all to spend them on. The "dance bar" was vacant. Bed.

The next morning, a group of youngsters aged about ten or eleven pumped us for English souvenirs, and in readiness to swap had brought with them a stock of Jena programmes, bare-boned affairs comprising eight pages. I still have a handful of them today, relics of an abandoned era, names such as Wismut Aue and FC Karl-Marx-Stadt competing in a national first division. I gave one kid that month's *World Soccer* magazine. I can still see his face.

There were tears in Jimmy's eyes as we said our farewells on the platform. I believed we'd provided him with a diverting interlude. He took off his glasses to give them a wipe and presented a forlorn figure as he waved out the train. Later, amid those Gerstungen uniforms once more, I found it impossible not to think of those wretched souls who'd risked their lives in crossing from East to West; of those who'd dared to defect, leaving behind all their possessions, their parents, sometimes even their spouses; and of those who'd frantically hurled themselves at that Berlin Wall and been coldly exterminated. Those balloon heroes hadn't been the only escapees right now. A swimmer called Renate

Vogel-Heinrich, a former world record holder, had just been smuggled into Bavaria. "I could no longer live in East Germany. As a promising swimmer you are taken away at fourteen. Even your parents don't know what is happening to you," she told the press. "You don't know what chemicals are put in your food or what is in the injections they give you. Sport is a national prestige affair for the Communists, and we are merely guinea-pigs." Indeed. Anyone who believed that the footballers of Carl Zeiss Jena played purely for sport and were happy factory workers for an optical engineering company, in an ideal society, was under a gross delusion. So was anyone who believed in Communism. Life needs vigour, vigour needs a keen mind, keen minds need debate. Debate was prohibited in Honi's East Germany, and lives were trapped. The uniform gave my passport an exit stamp. Within minutes the air tasted fresher. Lardhead smiled.

1979 also saw Dynamo Berlin, the Stasi's – tangibly – favourite football team, win their first of ten consecutive East German Championships. That sequence, born blatantly of corrupt engineering – a process seen at its most cynical in the steroid freaks produced within the ranks of athletes and swimmers by GDR trainers and doctors – sat plumb with the accelerating falsehood of a wider ideal, but ended quite simply when Gorby's policy resulted in the symbolic collapse of the Berlin Wall. Carl Zeiss Jena had meanwhile been allowed to win the Cup in 1980 and actually reached the following year's European Cup Winners' Cup Final. Among those who first passed dazedly through the Wall in November 1989 might have been fans of Hertha Berlin, historically the city's most popular club. Unable to watch their favourites since the Wall went up in August 1961, they had latterly been forced to stomach that abomination of what remained of their abiding source of enrichment, their favourite game. The Emperor Augustus had recognised the value of providing circuses, not merely bread, for the people of Rome. The East German Reds had become so stupid as to even deny that where league football was concerned, unless the word 'circus' is taken in its derisive sense.

I revisited Jena alone in late September 1996, the train flying past the derelict sheds of Gerstungen. The Hotel International was no more. For my first night, I paid £85 at the very plush Hotel Esplanade on the edge of a marble-floored indoor shopping centre with sensitised escalators, boutiques in competition, and sleepily switched to CNN after catching the second half of Carl Zeiss Jena's televised second division match against Eintracht Frankfurt. The next morning I sat beneath a Bitburger parasol by the old town hall, drinking cold beer and counting satellite dishes among the burgher houses. I heard

American businessmen. Despite the cranes, Jena looked already renewed in the autumn sunshine, an old charm reawakened and polished. I walked much further than before, and saw how pretty its wooded outskirts were, their old mansions standing proud. Back in the centre, I saw discreet Italian, Turkish and Chinese restaurants. I drank in bars that reminded me somehow of Oxford. A travel agency – "Last Minute Tours Jena" – offered packages to the Canary Islands, Thailand and Miami. Trabants looked unusual in the heavy traffic.

By evening, wandering on, folk disappeared and actual lamp-posts were noticeably thin on the ground. Through the murk I came across loitering skinheads. Café-bars were shut. By the tiny square next to where the Hotel International had once been, there stood a decrepit Communist icon, its fresh posters featuring a fit-looking Honi looming large from behind the Brandenburg Gate and issuing invitations to "Ostalgie Nights".

Of all the unravelling I attempted on this second trip, one thing above all else remains an enigma. That some people could cutely have grown rich while others, insecure, fell by the wayside was predictable. That there should be an attitude problem between Ossis and Wessis was also understandable. There was resentment at the Westerners' superior self-esteem and competitive pressure, and, from the other corner, at the bailing out of someone else's ruined economy by a people who themselves were only slowly bottoming out of recession. For Jena to look Wessi by day but still quite Ossi by night was less straightforward. Reunification certainly wasn't uncomplicated. But after the shopkeeper, in her late fifties, had handed me my change, and I'd showed her a photograph from September 1979, she'd merely smiled softly and said matter-of-factly, "Siebzehn Jahre ist nicht lange hier." Not in the context of centuries, but I'd have thought these past seventeen years of her lifetime would have felt pretty contrasting. At least the postcards she'd just sold me were in full colour.

Chapter 7

Passion Play

Greece: Iraklis v Ethnikos Asteras 27/9/98

Normally, in England, most non-celebratory noise and animation among home supporters tends to be the preserve of a main mob, normally behind a goal, and among those there are many who join the sporadic chanting out of duty. Elsewhere inside the stadium, individuals here and there will pipe up in encouragement or dissatisfaction: some might even jump up, normally in moments of special grievance.

Normally, in England, when a local club's away game is televised, the odd neighbourhood pub might contain a few of its supporters, perhaps vociferous as the beer goes down.

When I visited Greece in September 1998, Salonika was abnormal.

One of the early Greek philosophers, born around 350BC, was Zeno, who sought to disprove accepted theory where time was concerned, using paradoxes to do so. Zeno also founded the Stoic school of philosophy, which held that a man seeking wisdom should be free of the influence of passion, unaffected by either pleasure or pain. Zeno would have found recruitment to that school less difficult at Alton Towers than among Greek football fans, although by 1998, whilst the latter would doubtless have preferred indeed to forget about time, Zeno would have recognised the particular paradox which highlights the utter eccentricity that is Greek football. For all its extreme passion in the stands, the lack of success on the pitch at both club and national level throughout its history sinks to an embarrassingly low degree: like a fridge despite the hot kitchen that envelops it.

Not only has Greece won bugger all, it has barely ever graduated to a platform from which it might do so. Only once have the final stages of the World Cup been reached, in 1994, when the team lost all three group games in the USA without scoring a single goal. Only once have the final stages of the European Championships been reached, too, in 1980, when Greece finished bottom of its group. Panathinaikos' 0–2 defeat by Ajax in the 1971 European Cup Final at Wembley represents the sole appearance by any Greek club in any climax to a continental competition. Unrequited love can barely be better expressed than in the denial that afflicts the Greek football fan. Although he, if not a supporter of a major club, has allowed the average league attendance to slump alarmingly in recent years – escalating admission fees, burgeoning live TV coverage and, by no means least, the plague of hooliganism, have all been instrumental – he is still rabid at heart. If indeed a fan of one of the domestic giants, he provides the most vivid backcloth of all for the startled gaze of those of us watching televised highlights of European ties. When Panathinaikos faced Ajax in the second leg of a 1996 European Cup semi-final (77,000 were present in Athens), and when Olympiakos went within a whisker of eliminating Juventus before 70,000 at the quarter-finals stage three years later, the sheer bedlam had a perverse beauty of its own, the raging flares unleashed by the deafening, bouncing hordes like some metaphorical mass orgasm, and certainly emblematic of the fire within. Chaos thus becomes positive in encouragement.

But negativity, in the form of violence, has also been rampant. Back in my boyhood, the earliest photographs that I saw of fans misbehaving (accompanied by text horror-struck at the fanciful idea of deterrents like fences ever being introduced to England) featured maniacs variously scaling such barriers, stuck in moats, or being suffocated by uniforms, and these images were invariably from either South America or Greece. The introduction of full-time professionalism around twenty years after that, as very late as 1979 – though this, after all, was the land that begot the Olympics and its once-amateur ethic – served to tribalise the excesses and multiply them. In 1993, Athens' Olympic Stadium management complained that during the previous six years football fans had destroyed more than three-quarters of its 74,000 plastic seats. This was so heeded that two years later AEK supporters, incensed at their defeat by Panathinaikos in the Cup Final, wrecked 12,000 of them in one brief orgy. That match had provoked the wearied Sports Minister George Lianis to demand particularly tough punishment by the Greek FA, for inflammation had blazed. AEK, five of whose players spurned etiquette by refusing to collect their runners-up medals, had their president banned from attending games for six months because of his comments about the referee – who was beaten up a fortnight later at Athens airport. Meanwhile, when police visited a Panathinaikos supporters' club, they took away not only baseball bats and knives but also petrol bombs.

Shortly before my trip to Greece, a national newspaper's survey had revealed that fifty-two per cent of followers thought A' Ethnikis, the first division, was riven by corruption.

Those who holiday there in season – football's – and who might want to risk a different sort of dose – pandemonium – would find match day memorable. Particularly if a team of Salonika faces one from Athens.

I tend to categorise holidays into two kinds: 'exploring' ones and 'sunshine' ones. Whilst I find the first kind more enriching and the provider of much more lasting memories, I still like the second kind regularly, even though lying on a beach all day is definitely not for me. I don't crave a suntan, which fades tomorrow anyway unless you're shallow enough to sadly maintain it on a sunbed, and if I were to spend two-thirds of my time asleep I may as well be in Bartley Green, or perhaps the luggage rack of a train. On those occasions when I've had no choice in the matter, the best moments have been provided by a girlfriend indeed nodding off, enabling me then to enjoy a pedalo with only a few cans for company, and a sing-song a couple of hundred yards offshore.

What I do enjoy is the entire absence of any schedule whatsoever, in a reliably sunny climate and simply pleasant surroundings: and to rejoice in actually seeing and feeling that sunshine, perhaps on my own patio, maybe in a not-crowded bar or two right by the beach, with a book that transports me further over a leisurely drink or nine. And then see what the night might hold: hopefully, at the very least, balance. So, in September 1998, I went to tiny Fourka by the Aegean, not even bothering beforehand to be prepared by so much as a pamphlet, unaware that this Halkidiki peninsula had spawned Aristotle himself, and certainly that his father was doctor to Alexander the Great's granddad. I'd thought I'd read in the glow the latest offering by my favourite fiction author, Gerald Seymour, and hope, as you would, to get my leg over later. Ultimately I bemoaned that *The Waiting Time* – much of it set in the former East Germany – was very uncharacteristically dissatisfying, but much more quickly realised that Fourka, though a truly lovely resort for relaxation despite its yelping dog packs, held fuck all for any bedroom opportunist. Nicely, there were no Bolton shirts, or ageing Yorkshirewomen loudly comparing tea prices, or pushchairs; but everywhere were thirty-something couples, one member of whom, on my very first day, sat on a low wall by the pizza restaurant-bar La Strada talking office to London on his mobile. Some getaway. On my fourth day I got talking to Helen, who worked in a small supermarket, making an effort to meet her awkward English with the odd awkward Greek word I'd picked up. Tomorrow, drink? Yes, but also with friends, because people will talk. OK. Tomorrow, eleven-thirty at night, presented a fat, hairy-faced old woman sat on the till-seat, glaring. My mother says no. On the sixth day, Seymour read and penis irrelevant, I set out for Salonika. So in the end I explored anyway.

I had to change buses twice after starting at half-nine on this dazzling and already baking Sunday morning for the journey northward through the forested hills and terracotta-topped villages of Macedonia, surely indeed one of the most historically significant areas on earth. This was where, at Philippi, a momentous battle had been fought between rival Roman factions after Julius Caesar's assassination that would enable its victor, Octavian, to sweep away the republican ideal and create the Roman Empire. Philippi, also, through a visit by St Paul, became the first city in Europe to embrace Christianity. Macedonians, initially viewed from Athens as a mere bunch of uncivilised hill tribes, would come to exert upon Greece – and the world – an influence so profound as to almost defy estimation. After Philip had unified the nation his son Alexander, in attempting to conquer the whole of the known world, at least exported Greek culture, whilst Aristotle was the daddy of western philosophy, particularly logic. And much of our own present-day consciousness is represented by Mount Olympus, home of the mythological Greek gods.

That mythology had it that the world was shaped out of a huge jumble called Chaos (other words we owe to the ancient Greeks include democracy and tragedy). Nowadays, ironically, Macedonia – once pinpointed by Bismarck as the key to the Balkans themselves – is still chaotic. For a start, part of it is beyond Greece. In the eternal tinderbox that is the Balkans, Macedonia seems emblematic, should even that be possible amid such a regional jumble of centuries' ethnic conflict, religious feuding, vendetta mentalities: clannish, aggrieved minds, exacerbated by artificial frontiers that are largely the imposed legacy of invading imperialism, with dispossession of territory and oppression of – and agitation by – dispersed peoples. As the old Ottoman Empire collapsed, Macedonia became the objective of the two Balkan Wars that immediately preceded World War One and years later Tito would proclaim the portion that had been awarded to Serbia as a socialist republic. With the collapse in turn of the federal Yugoslav state, that portion declared its full independence in early 1992: a nation lacking any coherent identity, comprising Orthodox Macedonians, Muslim Albanians (despised by the former) and Serbs, and with no legitimate claim to its intended title of indeed Macedonia, a pronouncement that inevitably provoked uproar in Greece. The threat of eruption amid the Balkans, having been there always, will never die in my lifetime. Its unforgiving peoples have been pissed about so much for so long as to make Zeno look stupid. It'll take more than any Washington policeman or Downing Street college scarf. In April 1999, polls revealed that ninety-seven per cent of Greeks thought so, too.

"Fuck Aris" was my greeting, sprayed thickly across a wall, as I alighted after almost two hours in Salonika, capital of Greek Macedonia and Greece's smart second city, historically a strategic port that had survived both major fire and earthquake that century. Apart from being the birthplace of Kemal Atatürk, father of the modern Turkish republic (!), the city is home to four football clubs, Aris being one of them. The exceedingly friendly young barman across the road from the bus terminus, who spoke surprisingly good English and would point me in the direction of Iraklis' stadium, told me that sixty per cent of Salonika's football fans supported PAOK – his own team – and that Aris, the city's second most successful club, was ..... disliked. But not so much as any side belonging to Athens.

As long ago as 1906 a game between teams representing Greece's two major cities had descended into violence. In 1995 a drawn match between PAOK and AEK had produced so much injurious turmoil in the stands that the latter's coach, former Yugoslav international Dusan Bajevic, had called it a "crime against soccer" and warned that the government must take urgent steps to deal with this rivalry. In March 1998, Olympiakos players would need to evade rocks chucked by Iraklis supporters pained by a home defeat.

Iraklis' opponents this late afternoon were the newly promoted Ethnikos Asteras: of Athens.

I took a route to include the picturesque, broad waterfront, where an endless succession of stylish café-bars and a teeming pavement suggested that the entire population of 750,000 might be out enjoying themselves in the sunshine. What on earth happens to Greek females as they grow old? The stare of Helen's mother had been returned, not through distrustful denial but because I'd been astonished that her daughter could share blood relationship. Here, on Leoforos Nikis, were countless chic, beautiful young women, to whose male friends I showed the rudest of impatience when I closed my eyes.

Turning left away from the front by the fifteenth-century White Tower, an infamous scene of slaughter by Turks of teenaged Christians, I came across a neighbourhood of boulevards, rich greenery, tall modern structures, and more scrawled exhortations to screw PAOK's city rivals. Strolling on, other graffiti came to exalt "IRA". Eh? No, merely an abridged celebration of Iraklis. I sorely needed another drink as the sweat saturated my T-shirt and lubricated my legs, but by the moment I spied the Kaftatzoglio "National" Stadium all bars seemed to have dried up. Just around a corner, though, I found one, and felt almost to be gatecrashing. A party involving the best part of a hundred had commandeered the place, four colourful, raucous generations amid the balloons and flowers variously scurrying, shuffling, scoffing, slurping and occasionally snogging as the pavement strove to contain them a harmless arm's length from expensive-looking transport. Fourka's this scene was not.

Although no Greek footballer features in any *Who's Who* of worldwide all-time luminaries, a handful have begun to make varying degrees of impact abroad recently. Nikos Machlas banged home thirty-four goals for Vitesse Arnhem in the 1997–98 Dutch season to become the first Greek to head Europe's scoring charts, and Nikos Dabizas, a central defender for whom Newcastle United paid Olympiakos £2 million, became the first Greek to appear in an FA Cup Final. Donis, Zagorakis and Borbokis have all turned out in England's top flight. Experience gained in foreign leagues of higher quality can only be beneficial towards improving the national side's performance, whilst another boost came in 1998 when the under-21 team actually finished runners-up in the European Championship. But the domestic game has a serious financial problem. Within a few months of my visit, the government's Under-Secretary of Sport Andreas Fouras was threatening to bypass the Greek FA to rationalise the "nonsense". "The country simply cannot afford seventy-two professional clubs." The *Ta Nea* newspaper estimated that between them debts had increased to £55 million. Today's match in the Kaftatzoglio would feature no player who looked capable of sparking the national team or, through export, boosting his club's bank balance to a significant degree, whilst the size of the gathering underlined Fouras' concern.

The modern stadium's capacity – this was where a 45,000 full house had witnessed Bobby Robson's first victory as manager and Bryan Robson's first match as captain when England won a European Championships qualifier 3–0 back in November 1982 – enabled my transposition from the bar bash to a speck high behind a goal in ten minutes flat. The jam of parked cars allowed by the airiness of the surroundings confirmed that a match was indeed on, but I'd seen more pressing late rushes over dogs in Ladbrokes than at the ticket booth here. A quaint sight was that of rather tough-looking young men carrying little slices of polystyrene, whose sale I'd ignored, and which could only have been cushions. It was surely a mere compulsion of habit. The stadium was indeed a coverless concrete bowl, but aside from the sun's rays failing to singe my own arse, hardly anyone would ever sit still after five o'clock anyway.

For £5.30 – a cheaper option – I sat at the very top for a perfect view of the action. Behind me an estate of tall, white flats looked out over a tree-clothed park, away to my right a motorway cut through rolling green hills, but when I stood up to trail my eyes leftwards was the prettiest view of all, a panorama of the city as it pressed against the sparkling blue Thermaic Gulf, craft idling in the tranquil waters. Before me, though, whilst my own end was busy, lay a largely deserted stadium. Only another 3180 had parted with their drachma. If any of those were from Athens, they were hiding.

I quickly realised two things: that the standard of football was very poor indeed, and that I was in the company of maniacs. So early in the season, the match obviously wasn't vital, but the outpourings from around me – and visibly from everywhere else – brought to mind Shankly's immortal observation. The complexion of the game itself, littered with fouls and play-acting (it would stretch to 105 minutes!), and fragmented also through sheer lack of quality and consequent error, was one of Iraklis pushing on virtually throughout, at least on the floor. Only two players on the pitch stood out, and not simply because they were Zairean. According to *Ta Nea*'s inconvertible squiggles, their names appeared to be Xáykav and Mokóyko, the latter defender looking robust, self-composed, mobile and alert, albeit in the face of an Ethnikos pudding, whilst the former was the only forward on view who looked confidently quite sharp. They were both luckier, plying their trade here, than a compatriot had been three years earlier: when Mugade Cjimaga fell ill during a third division match, no doctor or ambulance were present, and he'd died.

Having struck the bar with a first-half free-kick, Iraklis rattled it again five minutes after the interval with a nipped header from Xáykav's cute cross. Midway through the second half the pressure finally looked as though it might achieve a breaking of the visitors' hopeful doggedness. A couple of minutes after their 'keeper had smartly kept out a low snapshot, Xáykav invited another clear attempt, blazed over to contortion of mind and body in the stands, and seconds after that an Ethnikos player was shown his second yellow card.

It would be facile to say that this increased momentum on the pitch was mirrored off it. Though they now indeed sensed a breakthrough and upped the volume still further, the fans had been barmy since the first whistle and didn't need any upped tempo on the part of their team to ignite them. If there were any reflections, they were players.

I've never elsewhere experienced fanaticism to such an intense degree. I was enveloped not by bodies but by bared souls. These folk were up for their football in a big, big way. The noise generated by so few was extraordinary and virtually continuous, choruses galore taken up by everyone, while everywhere people shot up to berate the heavens, hold their heads and shake their fists. During the second half the linesman away to my right signalled dubiously for offside. Not only did the five hundred on that side seethe in one mass tantrum, a ballboy in front of them, having jumped to stamp his feet half a dozen times, went apeshit in the official's face. One of those Greek words I'd previously picked up was *malakas* and this was screamed countlessly here, particularly at the very occupied referee who was certainly not favouring the home side, something Greek officials are often accused of. Paolo di Canio, who inexcus-

Iraklis playing Ethnikos Asteras

ably and infamously invited an English counterpart to collapse upon the Hillsborough turf this same weekend, would recognise the sentiment. *Malakas* means 'wanker'. Nobody else was chuckling.

Ever since Greek football was born, the imbalance between three Athenian clubs and the rest of the country has been striking: only six times between them have the rest been champions. Formed the same year as Panathinaikos, 1908, Iraklis – Salonika's oldest club – have merely one cup triumph to their name. The notion elsewhere that those three teams enjoy favouritism is certainly true in terms of investment, for it is presidencies there that attract millionaires and their pulling power.

Though barely an afterthought in comparison with Panathinaikos, Olympiakos or AEK, Ethnikos Asteras provided a moment now that somehow epitomised the ascendancy taken for granted in the capital and loathed in these parts. With a quarter of an hour left they broke upfield to the far end, a long high cross from the left sailed into an almost vacant penalty-box, and their gangling centre-forward leaped to loop a header over a sad goalkeeper in no-man's land. The ball struck his right post and rebounded into his net. Total, disbelieving hush.

I noticed an odd sign of resignation a couple of minutes later after Iraklis –

with Xáykav again the provider – missed an absolute sitter from close range. Cardiac peril had ebbed into wry smiles among a group of half a dozen mates – five now seated – a few rows in front. But the standing one also noticed this and promptly bent over to thunder and brandish his contempt, his face a knot of hurt. He certainly wasn't alone. The air by now was a pistol short of murderous. I heard enough *malakas* to rattle all of Japan.

It could only have come from Xáykav. Seven minutes from the end he capped a mazy solo run around the puddings with a low rasper that – also via a post – rippled the net. In that moment Iraklis saved the European Cup, recovered the rest of Macedonia, got their fantasy into a late-night taxi, and bombed every bank in Athens. I felt especially pleased for that young chap in front.

There was still time to spurn at least one gilt-edged chance of victory and further damage leather soles, but at the final whistle Ethnikos' ten were joined by their bench in ecstatic celebration of their unlikely point as the locals enacted dying embers. One other player who'd been conspicuous was now amid the dancing and hugging. The visitors' number twenty-eight, whose name certainly wasn't worth deciphering, had been the splodgiest pudding of all: a defensive midfielder, nominally, he'd highlighted his overall ineptitude within a fifteen-second spell during the second half, going to ground needlessly three times in a quick succession of failed tackles, ultimately left indeed sold on his arse as Iraklis poured behind him. He wore white boots! *Malakas*.

I was in no rush afterwards, but hadn't intended my leisurely stroll to become a disorientated stumble with the city centre's grid of roads now beyond dusk as well as recognition. Though traffic was quite heavy, not many people seemed to be walking the pavements. Bars, however, were packed: and in every one, chairs neatly arranged for the purpose, were rows of young men glued to a television screen. The taxi driver I eventually flagged down had his radio tuned in to the same happening. As he drove me towards the bus terminus I saw many more bars that could have been each other or the ones I'd walked past. Back inside the one I'd been in at midday, now solid too and not a female in sight, the same pleasant kid working the bar, here it was: PAOK, away in Athens, playing against Ethnikos Piraeus. They'd been trailing by the only goal when I walked in, by the look of it to another dreadfully poor outfit, making me wonder how on earth PAOK could have knocked Arsenal out of Europe the previous season. Fifteen minutes from time, though, the place shook with an equaliser. The barman, aglow with sweat and joy, negotiated the mayhem to bring me another bottle, this one on the house.

As I sat on the pool table and looked around, even though I wasn't inside any stadium at all, I still felt that I was living football through the special company of its most passionate followers.

But so it goes on. Later that 1998–99 season, the clubs staged a three-week strike in December when the government refused their demand for a bigger slice of the state-run football pool. PAOK were ordered to play five home matches on neutral ground after a pitch invasion when the referee denied them a penalty against Olympiakos – and their fans protested by blocking a major motorway. Five Aris fans were each handed a five-month jail term after their team's cup defeat by Olympiakos was held up for half an hour as rocks were thrown at police. Yet more seats at the Olympic Stadium were uprooted to chuck at police when Panathinaikos lost to Olympiakos, prompting yet another plea for corrective government action from the former's president George Vardinoyiannis – who in early May traded punches himself when a brawl broke out in that stadium's VIP section during a match against AEK.

Perhaps one story more than any other, though, sums up the domestic Greek football scene.

Back in 1988 Larissa were sitting three points clear at the top of the table in mid-March when their Bulgarian forward Georgi Tsigov failed a drugs test. Punishment came in the form of the club's being docked, calamitously, four points, which was highly convenient for AEK and others in pursuit. The townspeople massed in their thousands to demonstrate against what they saw as sheer sabotage of this tiny provincial club, and, as perpetrated by those PAOK supporters a decade later, highways were barricaded. Ultimately Larissa's only league title was saved when, although the club was fined and Tsigov banned from playing in Greece for two years, the decision to deduct the points was revoked.

Chaos.

Chapter 8

Stadium of Plight

Chile: Universidad de Chile v Osorno 24/9/94

Despite there being a mind-boggling 2,084 volcanos in Chile, its most memorable eruption for football fans came not from any lava outlet but from the snapped temper of a left-winger called Leonel Sanchez. However, whilst the national stadium in Santiago thus became momentarily a boxing ring for an infamous encounter during the 1962 World Cup Finals, it would provide an infinitely more injurious arena a decade later, where conventional sport was nowhere on the agenda.

That Chile's geographical statistics should throw up a curious figure or two shouldn't be so surprising. After all, its fundamental geometry makes it surely the most eccentrically shaped land on earth. Though more than 2,600 miles long, its breadth rarely extends to more than one hundred miles, this sliver by the Pacific stretching from arid desert in the north to glaciers in the south. It was in the north that I was introduced to this so diverse country, carried there by a marathon feat of endurance on the part of someone who was nothing less than a hero.

I'd been loath to leave Bolivia, probably South America's poorest nation economically and socially but, despite much squalor, its richest for spectacle and experience. A first, dramatic panorama of its capital when, through the trees, it came to reveal itself clinging to its Andean basin as the microbus ferried me downward, breathless, from its airport 13,000 feet above sea level; the weird bowler hats of the waddling Aymara Indian women; the peña where I'd knocked back wine into the small hours, enraptured by panpipes; the late afternoon sun twinkling so gloriously upon deep blue Lake Titicaca that thoughts of Incan past and champagne present melted into one sailing sensation of sublimity; the slow march of massed peasants protesting against government plans to curb their only livelihood, the growing of coca; women breastfeeding on buses that negotiated uphill hairpin bends on rocky tracks halfway to the heavens, with no barrier to save us from the ravines below. Indelible. Now, at five-thirty in the morning, I was at the main terminus in La Paz awaiting another bus to take me to Chile.

Peasants' protest, La Paz

Several coaches, looking modern and comfortable enough, lay parked up, but since no front window bore any destination sign nobody had any idea which of them would be setting out for Arica. Eventually two shirt-sleeved young men, bearing the look of drivers despite their absence of uniform, led the way through the gloom: past the coaches. I couldn't believe my eyes. What they opened the door to had possibly plied the Derbyshire Dales fifty years before. Was this small, rickety lame duck to make it across the southern altiplano without disintegrating? I climbed aboard, discovered not only that again I couldn't smoke but also that there was no toilet, and prepared for my demise to provide another cross by some dirt track, though whether that would be caused by ravine rolling or undiscovered starvation was up for conjecture. Twenty minutes out of the terminus the duck detoured for minor repair and extra fuel. I was in the lap of the gods.

In all my life I have never seen a book so ill-judged by its cover. The duck was Nobby Stiles and Alan Ball rolled into one: as a player, anyway. As its manager, the driver was Ramsey. An idea of the terrain can be gauged by the fact that although the distance between La Paz and Arica is only a couple of hundred miles, this journey would take the best part of a day. Treacherous mountain tracks, bumpy bleakness, waterlogged pits, rocks, past laughing llamas, parched desolation, unmarked routes occasionally denied by mineral works' jobsworths necessitating backtracks across those devil's contours once thought conquered: no wonder there were two drivers. But all the so-thought relief driver did throughout was change the tape and bring round some taste-less biscuits. For nineteen hours of intense concentration – with a handful of stops to smoke, munch and piss – the same sole person, surely no older than twenty-five, held the wheel. If he'd thought that the cat's-eyes and tarmac of northern Chile would provide a pansy's luxury as he now dealt with his final, tortuous Andean descent, a further challenge lay in thick fog. Seated directly behind me was a pair of English gap-year students. I heard one wake up to whine, "Isn't this simply the worst journey that you've ever had?" Gap year? Or gap life?

The driver beggared belief. When I staggered out into Arica at twenty min-utes past midnight, I had an intense regret that my now useless Bolivian money amounted only to perhaps two quid. After pressing it into his hand, I eluded the gappers.

Only twelve miles or so from Peru, Arica had been the desert port where Chile had agreed to place its northern boundary after its victorious expansion-ist War of the Pacific against Peru and Bolivia between 1879 and 1883. The desert in question was the Atacama, so dry that in some parts rain has never been known, but rich in nitrates and copper. Described by one traveller around that time as "a bleak, comfortless waste", Arica's size and population grew with international trade. Today it provided comforts that were bright and modern; aside from its proper roads, smart restaurants and neon-lit buildings, I saw that many of the populace were not only disposed but also well able to clothe themselves fashionably, European influence to the fore. A contrast with the Bolivia I'd just left recalled how I'd felt a few months previously when re-turning to Corfu from impoverished Albania. A plush seafood restaurant by the sunny Laucho beach provided an agreeable afternoon's lounging, my first sight of the Pacific Ocean, before I took myself to a site that belonged to my boyhood. Football is Chile's most popular sport – as that chariot had ap-proached Arica, I'd noticed kids playing on a floodlit all-weather pitch at a quarter to midnight – and this remote city had been a stage for those World Cup Finals of thirty-two years earlier. To its stadium, I had to go.

That same evening I'd caught on television the second half of Chile's home friendly against none other than Bolivia. The boys from beyond the mountains had triumphed 2–1 and the entertainment had been enhanced by a rotund stu-dio presenter with an extraordinarily orange complexion and a liking for hilar-iously pregnant pauses. But there was no match here. Instead, the ground played host to a festival evening of folklore, which disappointingly didn't feature those tinny brass bands, always curiously one note off-key, I'd seen parading through the streets earlier. The gallery of a few hundred behind one goal watched appreciatively, but for myself I have to say that it provided the biggest load of dross I'd seen on a pitch since the fag end of Bobby Gould's reign at the Albion. A few weeks later archaeologists would confirm that tens of mummified bodies, found across the city in ancient Indian burial sites by workers laying water pipes, predated Egypt's by more than three thousand years. A local museum, the San Miguel de Azapa, which displayed them, was risking their disintegration. Perhaps some of those mummies had somehow been alerted to their new predicament, had taken their leave, and joined in here. The folklore consisted continuously of several trance-like figures merely moping around in olden apparel, forever stooping to mimingly pick up sod all from the turf before shaking hands, to the grating accompaniment of a violin suffering a nervous breakdown. Agog with indifference to this unfathomable symbolism, I surveyed the ghostly scene beyond the artificial light.

This was where a gypsy genius playmaker called Dragoslav Sekularac had performed so marvellously for Yugoslavia that his vanquished Uruguayan opponents had themselves chaired him from the pitch. Here the legendary Lev Yashin had conceded four goals, one direct from a corner, in an extraordinary drawn game between the mighty USSR and unfancied Colombia, the former being pegged back from a three-nil lead achieved inside the opening eleven minutes. Yashin had also been at fault, beaten by two long-range shots, in a quarter-final lost to the Chileans, an unexpected triumph beheld by 17,000 fanatics representing the increasingly fervent mood of the host nation.

The size of that crowd is significant, for Arica's stadium was indeed a tiny bowl, uncovered too save for an unextensive backless roof to its main stand, where the concrete was now in sad decomposition. A monument behind that stand commemorates the staging of those Finals, but it also somehow testifies to the irretrievability of a long abandoned era. The football played in the 1962 World Cup was often violent and Ferenc Puskás would decry its defensive nature, but that tournament still had an innocence compared with today. The Czechs reached the Final without a qualified masseur, whilst England not only came without a doctor but also allowed an Australian millionaire to join their practice games. In a more profound context, though, it was an age when football's dog was as yet unwagged by its commercial tail. Sponsorship, marketing strategies, television clout and dollar signs aside, World Cups of today are decidedly not held among just four sites as was Chile's – three within a sixty-mile radius with the other a thousand miles distant – and, with the exception of Santiago's, not in stadia so miniature.

1962 saw John Glenn become the first American to be sent into orbit (some might wish for his homeland's all-pervasive culture to now follow a similar path); the most voluptuous woman ever to walk on earth, Marilyn Monroe, did so no more; Decca, considering that guitar groups were on the way out, rejected The Beatles. Also remarkable was that Chile should have staged the World Cup at all. Impoverished in those days anyway – highly unflattering pieces by Italian journalists would provoke ninety minutes' mayhem – its dubious capacity to provide the necessary infrastructure had been further threatened by a major earthquake even as Carlos Dittborn, the Football Federation's president, was arguing for the nod from FIFA. But it was South America's turn, Argentina had shown disloyalty to the competition in the past, and Dittborn's pledge of dependability despite the problems was accepted. When he'd pleaded that Chile must have the World Cup "because we have nothing", perhaps a few heartstrings were tugged too. Sadly, Dittborn himself would not survive to see his nation's finest footballing hour, its achievement of third place; ironically, his widow gave birth to his son on the very day that the USSR were defeated in Arica.

Sadly also for Chile, Dittborn's words could almost apply still today to an honours list at either national or club level. Since its Federation was formed in 1895 with British influence, Chile has always been a poor relation of the continent's triumvirate of Argentina, Brazil and Uruguay. It actually took Chile forty-two attempts over half a century to finally record a victory against Argentina. The premier club trophy, the Copa Libertadores, has only once been lifted since its inception in 1960 by a Chilean side, when Colo Colo triumphed in 1991. The Championship for national teams, first contested in 1910, has never been won by Chile, though they have managed to reach four finals. Other than in 1962, they have barely engaged World Cup historians. A ludicrous attempt to hoodwink those blocking their passage to Italia '90, when goalkeeper Roberto Rojas claimed to have been incapacitated by a firework during a qualifying match against Brazil, and the entire team walked off the Maracana pitch in protest and the hope they'd be awarded the points, provided their sorriest hour. FIFA proved that the firework had landed feet away, sussed that the apparent blood on Rojas' stretchered, feigning self had been the product of a burst capsule, and banned Chile from World Cup action until the 1998 qualifiers. Any whiff of corruption in 1962, though, was confined to exorbitance on the parts of hotel managers, agencies, and those who priced match tickets beyond the reach of most of the working class. These aside, Chile's delivery of the tournament was largely up to the mark, and the team's defeat of Yugoslavia to marvellously secure that third spot was understandably a cause of massive celebration.

My time available was insufficient to tour as much of this country as I desired to, but whereas the eerie, forbidding grandeur of its sub-Antarctic region thus pricked from afar only my imagination, there were serene landscapes to caress the eye within my compass. Serenity is probably absent from many people's perhaps vague conception of Chile, but – at least while its volcanos remain at worst smouldering – this can be experienced abundantly in the Lake District, an area of such natural beauty that had Wordsworth seen it he may have made an envious comparison. In fact, had Wordsworth ever arrived he would probably have been promptly slain, because this area had been the ancient homeland of the Mapuche Indians, fierce enough to resist not only the Incas but also the Spaniards themselves. They were appeased only in 1883 as the once small, compact Chile expanded southward too. Puerto Montt, nestling in the Golfo de Reloncaví 600 miles south of Santiago and middle-Chile, proved an ideal base from which to explore this verdant land of timeless forests and trickling waterfalls, azure waters and dramatic snowy peaks; and of an incongruously Alpine-like architectural heritage provided by immigrants towards the end of the nineteenth century. In the picturesque town of Villarrica – a nearby volcano actually erupted as recently as 1971 releasing thirty million cubic metres of lava, though it still features a popular skiing centre – I sat inside the busy

Shooting practice in the Lake District

Treffpunkt Club Social one night to hear only German being spoken: and, albeit half-cut, wondered who else might just have passed through half a century earlier .....

Chile, though few seem aware, possesses a myriad of attractions – some idyllic – for the adventurer. Even for more conventional tourists, its Pacific beach resorts of La Serena and Viña del Mar would certainly appeal. It was in Viña that I saw another heritage, English this time, and, of all the stadia ever chosen to host World Cups, surely the prettiest.

Situated in a bay like two peas in a pod, Valparaíso is Chile's second largest city, a major port, and actually seat of the National Congress, while Viña is the Ciudad Jardín: Garden City. Much affluence is here (plus a chance to blow it all in a huge casino), but the grassy landscaped squares, fountains and palm trees soothe away feelings of envy at the white mansions. The South American Film Festival was being held while I was there, but as an alternative to black ties there were black knickers to be seen in a handful of free-entry girlie bars where a drink for the lady was six pounds. Although Suzanna from Taiwan was genuinely beautiful, a cigarette was the sum total of my largesse while I contented myself – my wallet, anyway – with a small, inexpensive beer or two. As throughout all my travels around South America, there was no aggressiveness here. The only noise was being made by a party of Yanks on shore leave, one or two of whom disappeared upstairs, thankfully not with Suzanna, whose statistics I hoped didn't extend to figure with Valparaíso's as the AIDS capital of Chile.

Three-quarters of a mile inshore lay the Estadio Sausalito, next to a miniature lake and surrounded delightfully by various trees nestling upon gentle hills, with the Club Hipico racetrack close by complete with its olde-worlde black and white timbered grandstand. This English sporting influence was not confined to man's four-legged friends.

Personally, I wouldn't like my club to owe its very name to a grander version elsewhere. I prefer uniqueness – if it weren't for some outfit in Brighton I'd have that totally – but there are many instances on the South American continent of founders bestowing titles from their homeland. Ecuador has Barcelona, Uruguay has Liverpool, Brazil has Corinthians. And Viña del Mar is the home of Everton, forever recalling that Brits gave football to the world. The game in Chile was born in 1889 when Englishmen formed Valparaíso FC, and of the nine clubs who established the Federation six years later most were likewise. Valparaíso now possesses a club named Santiago Wanderers – I saw minibus after minibus of their green-bedecked fans, horns tooting, setting out for a match at Union San Felipe – and there is much evidence of other European influences too, clubs bearing names such as Audax Italiano, Union Espanola, and Rangers Talca. Santiago also has Club Palestino, while Rancagua – where England progressed from their group in 1962 – has a team wonderfully called O'Higgins, recalling the illegitimate son of an Irishman who helped José de San Martín fight for Chile's independence from Spain and signed its declaration in 1818.

Though roughly the same size as Arica's stadium, little Sausalito was smarter and infinitely more charming. A long, wide concrete approach framed by willows and cypresses led up to it, while inside the open terraces had been sprucely and colourfully maintained with brushstrokes of yellow, red and blue. These were visible because a mere 1,887 people had turned up to watch the blues and yellows of Everton play, appropriately enough, the reds of La Serena. On a pitch once graced by Masopust and Gento, Suarez and Puskás, and by Pelé himself, the fare today was thoughtful but somewhat less than mediocre. Sunday morning miscued wellies – South American defenders, as a rule, don't hang around in clearing their lines – vied with usually failed attempts at extravagant midfield flicks – South American attackers are often given to showboating – as the most memorable feature. Very memorably of course, this had been the scene of England's 1962 quarter-final exit, a team containing Charlton, Greaves, Haynes and a young Bobby Moore succumbing 1–3 to the artistry of, particularly, Garrincha. This afternoon, as a dozen small boys quaintly concentrated upon playing their own game on a spare strip of grass between the cycle track and the perimeter fence, Everton survived a late scare to win 2–1 in warm sunshine. This was especially pleasing to an ageing couple in the stadium bar, both of whom were adorned from head to toe in the club colours and seemed intent upon getting plastered in another sense, too. Wonderful! But again it had strained credibility that matches of such crucial, global import had been contested in such a humble setting: despite the fact that when the Czechs reached the Final by defeating Sekularac's Yugoslavia here, only 5,000 bothered to attend.

An hour and a half's coach ride inland from Viña lies Santiago, home of the President, Chile's three biggest club sides, and a national stadium of unparalleled infamy.

Built for the World Cup, it quickly achieved notoriety during Chile's second group match. The Italians were already unpopular because of their appropriation of numerous South American players for their own national team. The die was really cast, however, by those two Italian journalists, one of whom heavily criticised the facilities, while the other, more offensively, slagged off the country as a whole with references to illiteracy, squalor and – like a red rag to a bull – the unattractiveness and dubious morals of Chilean women. Such insults were doubtless used off the pitch to whip the local population into a hate-filled frenzy designed to unsettle the Italian team for such a crucial game, whilst the Chilean players themselves abraded their opponents from the off. Only four minutes into the game the Italian right-back David responded to a spiteful dig after the ball had gone and Leonel Sanchez, for suggesting to the referee that David should be sent off, received a stiff finger from another Italian to the side of his face, unseen amid the melee, at which he collapsed. Not long afterwards, but not before Ferrini's had been the first dismissal in the seventh minute for another retaliatory kick at a sly ankle tap, Sanchez, jockeyed into the corner flag by David, and attempting a drag-back, held the ball between his feet while grounded, and David attempted to hack clear. When this hacking struck flesh and bone, Sanchez leapt to plant a famous fist on the Italian's face. David fell flat on his back; the linesman, feet away, signalled nothing to the unseeing referee; Sanchez remained on the pitch. Not so David. Before the first half was over he seized his chance for retribution, meeting a chest-high ball with a boot that followed through onto the back of Sanchez' head. Thus down to nine men, Italy conceded two goals in the second half, and even as the referee – the Ilford schoolmaster Ken Aston – walked off at the end of a wholly disgraceful match, punches and kicks were still being thrown behind his back. The D stream at their most unruly had nothing on the Battle of Santiago. For himself, Aston, who described the entire proceedings as "uncontrollable", was heavily criticised for a lack of authority: this might also be applied to certain BBC commentators who between them, after heaping all the blame on Italy here, would show naivety or disfavour or both twenty-eight years later as West Germany provoked Argentina.

That commentator in 1962 had implicitly called for Italy's immediate expulsion from the tournament. Eleven years later, through their refusal to fulfil a qualifying fixture in Santiago, another team would be deemed to have withdrawn from the competition anyway, and it was these events that would predominate my thoughts as I made my way to the national stadium.

My first impressions of Santiago had indeed been of grubbiness, but these too would prove later to have been the book-and-its-cover scenario. You don't find cheap London digs in Mayfair. I found mine in the somewhat Dickensian Calle París, a dingy cobbled sidestreet off the well-beaten track of the Avenida General O'Higgins, with a brothel that passed as the Hotel Lucy heaving two doors away. Pizzenelli, he once of Florence's *La Nazione* newspaper, would surely have told me so had he been there now as well. But Santiago and Chile have transformed themselves in the meantime. Without having the vitality of Buenos Aires, and certainly not the grandeur of Barcelona or the sheer character of Lisbon, Santiago is nowadays decidedly squalid no more, even though its fast river remains brown. A short metro ride to Salvador, for example, lands you in one fountained city area of high-class restaurants, stylish bars and fashion-conscious punters. A cable car ride down from San Cristóbal hill produces not only adrenalin but also a spectacular view of the whole Andean-rubbed city, looking good. Bars such as the huge Pub Licity, providing live musical entertainment, the Phone Box Pub, leisurely and candle-lit, and the Red Bar, just around the corner from my digs and open round the clock, help make Santiago a piss-artist's paradise. I habitually enjoy a Friday night session, and Santiago handsomely didn't let me down at all. And if Pizzenelli could indeed revisit to sample the city's smart coffee shops, though he might be displeased by their blatant sexism as a marketing tool, he'd be taken aback by the gorgeousness – including facially – of the scantily-clad temptresses at your service.

I was in Santiago the weekend before my time in Viña. On that same day as Everton's victory, Colo Colo and Universidad de Chile – together with Universidad Catolica, the big three – would produce a goalless draw before an attendance of no less than 65,516, forty-five of whom would fall foul of the meticulously planned policing I'd seen featured on television the previous evening. "They fight like animals – like the English!" a man in the Phone Box told me of Colo Colo's fans.

"Fuck you!" had shouted a passing Universidad de Chile fan at me (earning a suitable reply) just before I mounted the steps leading from the refreshment area into the seating at the Estadio Nacional. As I'd been unwittingly positioned, ticket in hand, outside the section reserved for visiting supporters, perhaps that was the reason for his undoubted Americanism. Verbal abuse in this place, at any rate, is nothing. Osorno, struggling near the bottom of the table, were the team visiting La "U", neck-and-neck with Catolica at the top, and I took my £8.50 seat high in the Tribuna Andes overlooking the halfway line as the teams appeared. The events of twenty-one years earlier were not readily assimilated at this point, my having been awestruck by the huge white peak behind me and, while devouring a spicy meat cob, being assailed by the beating of a huge drum away to my left, which would continue throughout. "U", formerly the club of Leonel Sanchez himself, were neat and purposeful in a one-sided match, clean despite a late Osorno sending-off for a rash challenge, and won 5–1. Ground-passing their way through sorry opponents, they emphasised their superiority in the second half. In the 57th minute, their number eleven smartly controlled a sharp forward ball into the box and lashed it home low into the corner. After 74 minutes, the same player whipped home a low shot from just inside the area, past a 'keeper who'd had no time to move. Twelve minutes later, the number eleven danced clear and crashed the ball high into the net. Upon being substituted three minutes from time, this assassin was applauded enthusiastically by the 12,446 present in the vast bowl. Three and a half years later, by which time he'd also terrorised Argentinian defences for River Plate, this player would electrify 65,000 at Wembley, scoring both of Chile's goals in their unlikely, grandly historic victory over England. The number eleven was a youthful Marcelo Salas.

After the final whistle, the fans drifting away, I remained for a last, lingering, reflective look, and still found it difficult to imagine. Eventually, a police officer approached and motioned me to leave. I felt pleased to be able to.

Chile today takes its liberal democracy for granted and, since the unimpeded birth of that new order in 1990, has achieved social stability and splendid economic growth. In 1973, things were different. The leftist Salvador Allende's coalition government had argued amongst themselves, the nation's politics had grown more volatile, inflation had soared, and society had become ever more polarised. The country was in a mess. Into this chaos, in a manoeuvre not unheard of in Latin America (and, as portrayed in the excellent 1982 film *Missing*, with the active encouragement of the USA: Allende had become increasingly close to Fidel Castro), stepped one General Augusto Pinochet. The military's violent coup d'état, on September 11th, caught the nation wholly unaware. The man in the Phone Box, whom I knew only as Alexander, told me that he was merrily watching television as the planes approached the presidential palace.

Pinochet's rule – an unforeseen seventeen years of it – had its positive side, laying the foundations of a more efficient bureaucracy and stronger economy, but the means by which it was applied were based upon terror. He lost no time in setting out his stall. Whilst Allende – whose grave in the Cementerio General is still today honoured by socialists – soon, apparently, committed suicide, official figures – and surely conservative ones – put the number of those disappeared or executed by the secret police as 3,172, as Pinochet ruthlessly crushed all opposition. An immediately convenient site to concentrate those opponents rounded up – real, perceived, or otherwise – was the Estadio Nacional. An estimated five thousand were dragged here. Many were tortured but lived to tell the tale. Many were shot in the head.

If such poor folk, victimised for their beliefs – some of whom must surely have been there eleven years earlier celebrating Eladio Rojas' winner against Yugoslavia – came out of the national stadium scarred for life, then the USSR came out of a related episode with less dignity.

Another bizarre event in this abominable theatre took place on November 21st 1973: Chile kicked off, found the net inside twenty seconds without the opposition touching the ball, and were awarded the match. This was because the opposition hadn't turned up.

"…..well known that as result fascist upheaval overthrow legal government national unity now in Chile prevails atmosphere bloody terrorism and repression … reigns wild provocative campaign against socialist countries and all democratic forces … National stadium supposed be venue hold football match turned by military junta into concentration camp place of tortures and executions … soviet sportsmen cannot at present play at stadium stained with blood of Chilean patriots …" These words helped form the determined message of a cable received at FIFA headquarters on November 3rd 1973 from the USSR Football Federation; the match they were refusing to participate in was the second leg of a World Cup qualifying play-off, which FIFA had ordered should proceed because the safety of the USSR party and non-intimidation of its players, upon investigation, had been guaranteed.

When the USSR refused to budge from their stance that the second leg must be played in a neutral country, FIFA raised the possibility of playing the match, whilst not in a third land, at an alternative Chilean venue, thus enabling the USSR to avoid the tainted stadium in Santiago. Viña del Mar was proposed. Still the USSR refused. All pretty rich, anyway, coming from a land that itself had perfected the use of labour camps and mass political purges, and had removed the word "democracy" from its dictionary.

The facts are: they'd been held to an unnerving goalless draw in Moscow in the first leg; and at a meeting between representatives of the Chilean and USSR Federations in Zurich on September 21st to discuss the organisation of the double-legged play-off – with the murderous purge in Santiago already ten days old, but prior to their failure to secure a satisfactory result at home – the USSR had made no mention at that point of any reluctance to play in Chile.

Thus it was that the USSR withdrew from the World Cup, thereby precluding any loss of face. Not only for the Kremlin's ideology, but also on the football pitch. Behind every wretch, an opportunist lurks.

As I left the stadium behind, I passed slowly through a neat, clean neighbourhood, its small houses lovingly maintained. I was bound to wonder whether any people living in them now had also been there twenty-one years ago and, if so, how they'd dealt with the sinister crack of gunfire behind their drawn curtains.

Perched on his bar stool with a Cristal beer on the Avenida Providencia, Alexander attempted an explanation of how the national stadium could eventually rediscover its true meaning following its dark, horrific episode. A symbolic blessing by the Pope had certainly helped, as had the in-built opportunities provided by the very stadium to the masses for airing their political opposition, particularly during the last days of the military régime (match days in Eastern Europe have provided similar rallying points over the years). And this by-product of protest, a partial exorcism, was of something that had belonged indeed to the early days of that régime. For over four years now, Alexander hiccuped, Chileans had enjoyed – and become accustomed to – the democratic rule of civilians. "We do not forget, but history is history." Time and the resilient human spirit can deal with most things. Hillsborough was not without its Liverpool fans once a season.

In September 1994, Pinochet remained as the unimpeachable commander-in-chief of the armed forces, which were still not under the control of the new order, though they were not perceived as dangerous to the successful political system. But by May 1998, a month after he'd stepped out of his uniform and into a lifetime seat in the Senate, bullet-riddled bodies, hands tied with barbed wire behind their backs, had been unearthed from the Atacama Desert, and a judge of the Santiago Appeal Court had bravely set in motion an inquiry as to whether Pinochet could now be tried for genocide: a matter, long drawn out, that would soon embroil even ourselves, when Pinochet's visit to England saw him controversially arrested to accommodate a Spanish lawyer's extradition demand.

In June 1998, meanwhile, Chile returned to the World Cup Finals stage – by virtue of beating Bolivia in their last qualifying match – and performed quite creditably in France, drawing all three group games, going within whiskers of beating Austria and old foes Italy, before bowing to Brazil in the second round.

But the chances of Santiago's national stadium again staging the most important game of football on earth would seem as remote as the likelihood of its re-enacting a death camp.

Chapter 9
A Coiffured Cheat

Spain: Hércules Alicante v WBA 14/8/77

"What's gooin' on ovver thier?" ejaculated Lionel Lamp-post. We all looked towards another table by the roadside. Seated at it was an immaculately groomed Spanish male, sharp black suit, bow-tie, clipped moustache, dark wavy hair. His company, two very attractive young females, enhanced the impression he gave of a smooth, swarthy playboy. Right now he had someone else for company, too, and this person was standing. The dialogue seemed very cordial, though aided by a liberal use of sign language. We all knew this fourth person, a certain short Scotsman. A pat on the shoulder from him, and the Spaniard beamed. A few words followed by a kiss-fingers-bellissimo gesture, and he displayed his keen accord. A few more illustrated words, a thumbs-up sign from the Scotsman, and the convivial Spaniard did likewise, still flashing his toothpaste grin. Then a smiled buenas noches from our hero, who lastly produced another hand-sign with which the Spaniard somehow couldn't have been familiar. Perhaps he thought it had something to do with his reward, who would doubtless soon accompany him to his hotel room. Emilio Guruceta Muro, supposedly the best referee in Spain, was nodding his head in complete, laughing agreement as Willie Johnston mimed something in front of his trousers.

Closer chuckles rippled into the Costa Blanca's balmy night air. One of them came out of Fat Denis's face, another from Farmer's. Not from long-haired Mick's, though: he'd have been back in hospital by this hour. Somebody else at our glass-full table had spent an awful lot of time in hospital too, despite his tender years. He was still feeling thoroughly disgusted right now. "We shoulda broken a few bloody legs," said twenty-years-old Bryan Robson.

Back in August 1977 Benidorm still had some way to go in its transition from a tiny fishing village originally settled by the Moors to a wholly slick mass-tourist trap, ultimately the Med's largest with four million visitors a year. In some ways it was nicer in those days: its less than perfect infrastructure – some streets were still pure sand – still allowed the merest pinch of authenticity, many more would-be publicans called John or Mary had yet to descend with their unimaginative menus from Pontefract or Oldham, and there was Abba to be heard instead of Aqua. Nor were the five of us, for that matter, on a package. After an evening coach journey from Alicante, we'd been fortunate to find digs. So we'd thought.

The Lamp – a lodger of Farmer who was five feet six inches of livewire and roughly of Mick's mould – had taken solace in the certainty of mattress and pillow after discovering that he stood little chance of realising here his predilection for coloured girls. Though indeed Anglo-Saxon, we always kidded him that he looked Afro-Caribbean himself, with his black curly hair and enviable year-round tan. This was the predator who was once overheard at midnight in a Dudley bus shelter by the rest of us – and everybody was standing, though not quite everyone was eating pie and chips – to reply to an entreaty of, "Yes, give me more, more!!" with the admission: "I ain't got no more ...."

The digs, a few rooms above their bar, belonged to a middle-aged couple from Blackburn. Salubrious they weren't. Because of the non-existence of air-conditioning, one of us decided at half-three in the ultra-humid morning to forego the mattress and doss on the landing. A scream quickly arose. The floorboards, rotten, had disintegrated. Below looked like a hundred-foot drop into the deserted bar. Digits had grabbed what they could, like lemmings having second thoughts. A creak, another frantic scream, and stained underpants among the gathered gallery. Eventually a hand, seemingly pissing itself too if hands could, offered rescue. One other hand should have attempted reach. Two did. The reluctant lemming shot away.

"Yo alroight?"

Any reply seemed somehow superfluous.

"Aw shit ....me leg...."

Not long afterwards the owners returned from walking their dog, which could hardly be called Rover because it was a Doberman Pinscher. A strident order was issued to congregate downstairs, which by now featured a broken chair, an overturned table or two, and a near-naked drunkard gurgling across the carpet. Arthur of Blackburn wasn't impressed. His wife, now holding the excited brute, was more observant.

"Arthur! Look!" Arthur's eyes shot upwards to blazingly survey the gaping hole in the ceiling, strands of timber sprouting forth like octopus legs.

"Fuckin' out, the lorra y'! An' I want another fifteen 'undred pesetas before y' fuck off, an' all! Now!" The dog looked hungry.

I thought, in hindsight, useless by definition, we might have made a few bob there ourselves.

We arose, from bags for sandy pillows, to a gorgeous Mediterranean mid-morning, with the sea glistening like gems beneath the scorching sun in a sumptuous blue sky. The parched Levante beach had already assumed its attraction for tan-seekers, gambollers, snoozers and posers, the promenaders were out in force, and the cafés were briskly in business, the Spanish waiters in their faultless white shirts and black bow-ties expertly performing their one-handed trick of ferrying at nonchalant speed full trays bearing coffee, orange and San Miguel. Above the straining heights of hotel blocks stood the stark outline of forbidding mountains, an abrupt contrast to the colourful playground below; but from all parts wafted the sound of music, and any cares were banished to oblivion.

Denis was baffled not so much by the huge red spots that had sprung up overnight to decorate his limbs and employ his fingernails on overtime as by the discovery that his shoes were soaked inside and all the more smelly too. Mick swiftly suggested coffee. That downed, and unblacklisted, we found somewhere else.

Spain perennially stages pre-season tournaments, which for visiting teams provide a refreshing change of environment after the slog of preparatory training and a competitive tune-in on the eve of the new campaign. This one, in Alicante, featured besides Albion the host club Hércules, Dynamo Tbilisi of the Soviet Union and SK Beveren of Belgium. Our opening game was against Tbilisi and we awaited this eagerly, especially since four of us had never before experienced the delights of following our team abroad and the warmth of spirit that comes with that. There's a sense of total escapism, of exploration, and of proudly flying the colours far from home. Mick, so much a fanatic that he'd once forked out for a taxi all the way from Dunstable to Carrow Road when his coach broke down, was taking things in his stride. Right now he strode to the toilet.

"So what toime's the kick-off tomorra?" asked Lionel as he picked at his salad.

"Half-ten," replied Denis in between mouthfuls of barbecued buffalo or whatever it was he was stuffing his face with.

"Seem weird watchin' the match at midnight, won'it eh?"

Denis fell silent, nudged by Farmer to cast his eye over a big black dog that had trotted airily up the pavement, sniffing this and that along the way, before arriving at the entrance to the bar, which was shaded by a tree. Denis grimaced at Farmer, who then nodded towards the absent Mick's beer glass. "Yer shoes OK now?" enquired Farmer. Sadly, the hound was too quick.

That afternoon we lazed on the beach, The Lamp hoping to turn from brown to black, and occasionally we'd break off from the heat and negotiate the lissom sprawl to muck about among the lapping waves. Sunshine, scenery, tanned blondes, cheap booze, football: life! Actually, it was almost Mick's death.

We hadn't paid much attention to the fact he'd spent hours flaked out with eyes closed, mouth open and making noises not unlike that of pigs copulating. Assuming he was content we'd left him to it, but really should have known better, because when he rejoined the world at six o'clock he mumbled that he felt terrible, and he could barely stand. We knew he was really in a bad way when he stayed in that night.

The following day his skin was so sore that the slightest touch meant agony. Wearing clothes was impossible. As he shambled around Benidorm he looked like a cross between some guru and an escapee from a mental home, for around his pinkness was a white bedsheet, and to spare any irritation his long hair was scooped into a bizarre bun, secured by a purple comb. Belying this somehow cherubic appearance, however, was the arresting sight beneath his naked legs of heavy black shoes which, were it not for their fashionably pronounced heels, might have been suited to rummaging around in a coal cellar. A topless Racquel Welch couldn't have turned more heads in the street, whilst the expressions on those faces that encountered him in the bars and souvenir shops ranged from unconcealed amusement to bewildered alarm.

Around five we caught the narrow-gauge train for its scenic journey along the coast, Mick forsaking the bone-hard seats to get down on the floor. The weather was oppressive and gnats abundant as we ambled around Alicante. A prosperous, stylish and essentially Spanish city, Alicante's profile of tall modern offices and apartments was softened by the lush palm features of its marble esplanade, its old warren-like Santa Cruz quarter where meandering pedestrians held sway over honking cars providing a quaint contrast to the bustle of modern commerce. Eventually we found the Estadio José Rico Pérez: smart, entirely open Spanish-fashion to the elements, and which five months earlier had staged its first international match when Spain and Hungary shared two goals in a friendly. It held around forty thousand but tonight was only a quarter full, enabling Mick to watch the action flat out on the concrete terracing, the image of a mortuary slab all the more vivid.

Curiously, whilst Hércules Alicante's honours board has remained bare – very unlike that of Valencia, not so very far up the coast – all three of their guests were soon to enter a splendid period in their history: or at least, in our own case, a splendid season. Within two years our potent, wholly entertaining brand of football would become the talk of the nation, although typically we'd be unable to translate this splendour into medals. Not so the others. Beveren, who'd lost 1–3 to Hércules the previous night, would win their only four trophies between 1978 and 1984, including the Belgian championships of '79 and '84, a prominent member being the much-capped goalkeeper Jean-Marie Pfaff before he was sold to Bayern Munich. Dynamo Tbilisi, meanwhile, would be Soviet champions for the second time in 1978, would demolish Liverpool in the first round of the 1979–80 European Cup, and in 1981 would become the only Soviet club other than Dynamo Kiev to lift a European trophy when they defeated Carl Zeiss Jena for the Cup Winners' Cup.

There was no Alexander Chivadze, Tengiz Sulakvelidze or David Kipiani tonight, but such absence didn't prevent Tbilisi from, in all honesty, playing Albion off the park, their display an antithesis of the common perception around that time of Soviet football (Kiev excepted), one of dour, unimaginative stodginess. Despite their having arrived in Alicante only a few hours prior to kick-off after a tortuous journey from their far-flung Georgian outpost, they were immediately into their stride and conviction. They were not just solid and dependable defensively, but thoughtful and polished in fashioning their attacks and elusively quicksilver at the sharp end – none more so than Vladimir Gutsayev, a wriggling, ubiquitous centre-forward whose balance, change of pace, feinting and dribbling made him a nightmare for John Wile, Ally Robertson and company. The rather better known forward Ramaz Shengelia particularly caught the eye, too. Tony Godden – "a vay-ry fine goalie!" enthused one local on the bus afterwards – had to pull out a handful of blinding saves.

And yet, for all that Albion were unable to pick up the thread of their own game, the only goal of the match was unjustly ours. The tall and bearded centre-forward David Cross took full advantage of rare slack marking inside the box to fire home low twenty minutes from the end.

It didn't really matter to anyone, but when I found out that Tbilisi subsequently stuffed Beveren 4–1 I felt pleased for them.

We took Mick into hospital. The staff made it known that we were bloody stupid not to have done so earlier, and their looks of disquiet unsettled us. With myself limping around on a seized-up knee (for it was I), we'd become a somewhat bedraggled lot.

"Bring 'em over, George," shouted John Osborne, our other goalkeeper nearing the end of a career that had seen him gain an FA Cup winners' medal back in 1968. We'd plonked ourselves at a vacant table surrounded by those bearing familiar faces: two distinct groups, one of portly gentlemen, not saying much, wiping their brows, viewing us warily, and the other of fit young men in T-shirts and slacks, their right arms more active in the still-crowded Friday night. We'd struck up a conversation with Alan Everiss who'd been Albion's secretary for donkey's years and whose father Fred had begun that family's unbroken association with the club, in one capacity or another, before the turn of the century no less. Mr Everiss was an amiable fellow, and when I'd asked whether George Wright, the physio, might look at my knee, he'd immediately fetched him, bless his heart. George had been drinking with the players.

"Fell through the ceiling! Pissed up, were y'?"

"Well ...."

"You were pissed up," grinned George.

When George duly transferred us into the other sector, there were Paddy Mulligan, Cross, Robertson, Johnston and Robson sat with dear old Ossie. Not surprisingly, they were still talking admiringly about the football of Tbilisi.

We sat down opposite Robertson and Robson. Lionel thought it was Robertson and Godden.

"Y'know, oi never realoised 'ow much yo look loike Bryan Robson," said The Lamp – to Robson. A tolerant smile.

"Pity 'bout Johnny Giles leavin', worr'it?" continued Tividale's twat diplomat, as Farmer gawped disbelievingly and Denis looked away, eyes rolling. Giles had dragged us up from the second division a year earlier, was considered something of a saint having also established us back in the top flight, but had recently quit to universal dismay.

"A' well," said Ally Rob while trying to catch the waiter's attention. "These things happen."

"This's what y'want," said the one who would become Captain Marvel elsewhere, when the tray arrived. "Gerr'into it!" And we all did.

"Wish we could go t'Benidorm as well," lamented Ally.

"Lerr'us know 'ow yer mate gets on," said John Osborne.

Those vacational joys provided by our remaining time in Benidorm were of the usual kind, though in my own case they threw up an ironic one. We all have our little foibles and a rather pathetic little ambition of mine has been to roar out the name of my homeland at the point of fluidic discharge into a Fräulein or, as I grow older, Frau. How inappropriate, then, that I should come to notice on the right shoulder of Karen from Manchester a tattoo bearing the name of Franz. Zambian, she said. Doubts remain. At least my knee survived the fitness test.

So: Sunday was the day of the 'Big Final'. Our first business back in Alicante was the obvious one, but they wouldn't let us see him and furthermore they told us he'd be in there for some days yet. We left his bag for him, and began to worry about not only how he'd get home but also how he'd pay the bill.

Awaiting the bill for our pre-match meal, though, provoked no impatience. A mosquito surprisingly visited Lionel's skinny lower leg, whereupon he managed to sweep his plate clean off the table, though not before it'd deposited half its paella over his turquoise and yellow shorts. The plate actually performed a wondrous semi-circle before clanking to a halt at the feet of a fellow diner, who resembled Queen Victoria. The Lamp's inadequate, table-jolting reflexes had meanwhile also succeeded in toppling Denis's drink, so that it nicely flooded his own steak and chips. Farmer, convulsed, now helplessly ejected a mouthful of masticated lasagne over the remnants of Fatty's feast. Poor Denis bore the look of an indignant bloodhound. "Yo barmy cunt!" he barked at Lionel, who'd bent down to pick up his plate, dark brown matchstick arms and legs all over the place, but his anus invitingly prominent. The commotion caused by Denis applying his size nines quickly brought out the restaurateur, who resembled Hattie Jacques.

It was while we were standing at a hamburger stall that we spotted through the throng something teetering towards us. God knows how, crazily, Mick had escaped. He was even wearing jeans and a top, and his hair had reassumed its customary design. The doughty superfan could hardly speak, though.

The noise generated by the gathering of 25,000 that would rise into the steamy night over the next couple of hours was unlike anything heard at St James' Park or Elland Road. Whereas English crowds' support tends to be a heavy, throaty roar assailing your eardrums like a mallet, this was of a shrill, screeching tone that lanced into your senses, like a pit of angered snakes. The massed locals were evidently taking it very seriously, their partisanship bordering hostility, and whipped up further by the incessant drum-bashing of a sombrero-clad character who looked a bit like Denis, still put out. Meanwhile, high away on rocks to our right, the imposing Castillo de Santa Bárbara that had stood guard for centuries seemed to haughtily disown this floodlit fervour and look instead towards the moonlit sea.

We were feeling pretty confident. George Wright had watched Hércules against Beveren and told us, "We'll beat 'em six!" A blast on the whistle of Guruceta, and we were away to a crescendo of shrieks. After ten minutes, a Hércules forward fell theatrically inside the box. It was probably indeed a foul, but the hammy histrionics and ready approval were a harbinger. Penalty. 1–0.

In the 39th minute Guruceta awarded another: this one was total bollocks.

2–0. Tony Godden vented his disgust by booting the ball as violently as he could upfield for the restart, so that it carried a few yards past the centre-circle. This was actually a much more accurate effort than his usual kicking performance that would engage row C forty yards out, but although he was hardly guilty of delaying the game's progress or of serious dissent, Guruceta felt sufficiently affronted to brandish ceremoniously – thus irritatingly – a yellow card.

The referee's overall mishandling of the proceedings in our disfavour had caused us to simmer with real rage. Big Wiley, our skipper – accompanied by the Spaniard concerned, admittedly – was sent off for nothing more than evasive self-defence when his opponent, Giuliano, reacted spitefully and chased after him following a hard but perfectly legal tackle.

When Laurie Cunningham – the most prodigious talent I've seen in forty years of following The Baggies, God rest his soul – somehow pulled a goal back on the stroke of half-time, the reaction was inevitable. Farmer and myself shot out of our seats and danced in the aisle, fists clenched in defiance. "Worr'about that then, ya bastards!" We were promptly greeted by not only a hailstorm of orange peel from hissing, teeth-bared natives but also an urgent call from Denis to, "Siddown, y'twats!" "What the fuck for?!" I bawled. "Fuck this!" Denis calmly pointed in the direction of the dugouts. A uniform was pointing a gun and smirking. We slunk back down, and didn't even ask Lionel if he'd experienced any special reaction when Laurie scored. Mick's wry smile, meanwhile, spoke volumes.

It was the 72nd minute that marked the point where blazing anger diluted into resignation and merely amused contempt. Hércules attacked up their right and a dangerous cross was expertly intercepted by teenaged left-back Derek Statham, who neatly breasted the ball down and scurried with it in one fluid movement out of harm's way. His reward was the spectacle of Guruceta, for the third time, loping towards the penalty-spot where he indicated handball, stroked his moustache, and checked his coiffure. Handsome beast. 3–1. Fix.

One of the great characters of British football – Johnston – was on our left wing. There was more than a touch of the devil in him, though in a mischievous rather than malicious way, so that a loud remark one afternoon at Upton Park of "you narsty little mane!" fell some way beyond the truth. His natural ebullience often involved playing to the gallery, and occasionally this would include the taunting of his immediate opponent by actively inviting him to attempt tackling. Now, he took the ball to within five yards of the right-back José Antonio, slowed to a standstill, and beckoned him forward to have a go. The Spaniard, whilst Willie was doing nothing against the rules, bore the expression of a seven-stone weakling arriving home to find the gasman servicing his wife: outraged, humiliated, powerless. Pained eyes flashed towards Guruceta. Yellow card for Johnston.

Immediately, Hércules scored a fourth goal, a proper one. Two minutes later – in a game of six yellow cards (five ours) and three real reds, all of this in what was essentially a friendly fixture – came the most maniacal moment of all. Ronnie Allen, all too aware of Johnston's enlivened mood, walked to the touchline for the purpose of substituting our darling demon. Guruceta easily flashed the manager a red before reality dawned. Poor Ronnie. His attempts to incur no further disciplinary comeback foundered straightaway when Mick Martin was expelled. There was no discernible reason other than I saw Guruceta screw his face before taking a deep breath.

In the final minute Albion's forever futile, dispossessed, nine men conceded a fifth – a brilliant, rasping shot by Verde – and that was that. The curtain fell on the farce. The trophy, a monolithic absurdity, was held aloft to rapturous acclaim and Mick's half-belch. The midnight air seemed absolutely, squalidly, burlesque. The Hércules players, no longer expectant, looked pathetic.

"Aarrhh, these're only fun games," soothed John Osborne. "The real stuff starts on Saturday." Whenever I think back to Bryan Robson's historic playing career, I always remember August 1977 and his total loathing to be second best.

We all went back, eventually, to the very plushy Hotel Gran Sol. The players had a drinking party lined up in its conference room; it was our own last night, too. The party, around the hugest of tables, lasted till half-seven in the morning, its conversation touching upon all sorts of things, some to do with football, others definitely not. Ice buckets maintained impulse. We picked a dream team. Johnston insisted upon Denis Law even if this meant tough shit for Pelé or Eusébio. Meanwhile David Cross, in his laconic way, told we four at least twice that Albion had been presented with a runners-up trophy the day before.

Crossy seemed as resigned, seriously, as Ally Brown was melancholy. Brown was convinced he'd played his last match for Albion the previous week in his native Scotland. He'd been squeezed out of the first team and didn't look like reclaiming his place. "Fancy playin' yer last game at Ibrox! What a place t'go out!"

"Where d'y'fancy, Ally?" mooted Cross. "D'y'think Stoke'd do us, eh?"

The club had recently acquired a big, coloured centre-forward who was destined to make his mark in a wholly electrifying manner very shortly: Cyrille Regis. But whilst Cross would indeed leave before long, Ally Brown's fears would prove groundless. Ron Atkinson, after Ronnie Allen's departure, would rightly see the crafty, strong-running Brown as the perfect partner for Regis.

"Ere y'are," said Len Cantello, hard as nails in midfield, very talented and professional with it, the kind of player all Baggies yearn for nowadays, and something of a hero to Bryan Robson. "See if y'can beat this." Licking a small coin, he stuck it on his forehead and proceeded to thrust his head downwards seven or eight times before the coin eventually fell off. "C'mon John, you now!" Cantello licked and placed it on Farmer's forehead: and without his knowing, immediately took it away. Farmer sat there triumphantly for a full minute nodding away like some deranged yes-man before he realised. Not to be outdone, he was soon challenging anyone to match his wedding tackle. Willie Johnston immediately shot up but was still fiddling with his belt as Farmer, coolly leaning back into his chair, plonked his right leg on the table. The joke shop purchase nestled against his ankle.

The morning newspaper arrived. "El West Bromwich Albion, un buen equipo, sin suerte anoche."

"What's that last bit mean?"

"Without luck."

"Very diplomatic."

Willie told us to make sure there were no bottles left lying around, to take them with us. The generosity of this paled into insignificance, though, when Mick told us the following Saturday that the club had paid for everything.

The next, and mercifully only other, time we came across Guruceta was in Jena two years later, but although we'd feared the worst upon incredulously being hit by his name in the match programme, our lamentable defeat in that UEFA Cup-tie had nothing to do with his dubious practices.

This wouldn't be the case for Nottingham Forest. In 1984 they went to Brussels with a 2–0 lead for the second leg of their UEFA Cup semi-final against Anderlecht. Paul Hart had a perfectly legitimate goal disallowed. A penalty decision against Kenny Swain was described by Brian Clough as "a travesty". Television footage proves both grievances. Anderlecht won 3–0. Thirteen years later their president, Roger van den Stock, would finally admit that his father and predecessor, Constant, had paid the referee, Guruceta, £18,000.

Instances over the years of bent refereeing – or of attempted bribery, at least – form a catalogue overspill. When the activities of Kurt Rothlisberger came under scrutiny in 1997, UEFA president Lennart Johansson winced, "This could be just the tip of the iceberg." Bernard Tapie, the infamous erstwhile

Sin indeed

president of Marseille, is estimated to have drawn upon a slush fund of £3.5 million to ensure suitable scorelines in France and elsewhere. English clubs have sadly, inevitably, been on the receiving end of such corruption. Whilst the Portuguese referee Lobo resisted an attempt to buy his favour for the second leg of the Juventus-Derby European Cup semi-final in 1973, Liverpool, for example, had been blatantly cheated when they similarly faced Inter Milan eight years earlier. And whilst the reaction of Leeds fans in Paris to their defeat by Bayern Munich in the 1975 Final, no less, was deplorable, those who so readily castigated them ought to have appreciated the cause.

Albion's experience in Alicante meant nothing in comparison, but for those of us involved it was still sickening. The worst thing in football, bar none, is to be cheated.

Guruceta died in a road accident in 1987. Poor car.

Chapter 10
Vanishing Acts

Hungary: Ferencváros v Pécsi MSC 6/6/92

The weather was in irritating mood. Much of the Budapest sky this early June Sunday morning was blue but the rain was insistent, and I tried to elude it by leaning tight against a press box inside the deserted, huge, virtually coverless stadium. For an Englishman, the place held but one thought. Below me was the pitch where, thirty-eight years earlier, Billy Wright, Tom Finney, Roger Byrne and the rest had been slaughtered 1–7. A few months before that, those executioners had electrified London with a surging mix of poetry and savagery, shocked us to the core with six goals, and thrown us from our smug pedestal onto the shingle of self-examination.

The rain relented and it was time to leave the Népstadion. They hadn't bothered sweeping it and my boots crunched on discarded nutshells, hundreds lying around from the previous Wednesday when Iceland had come here for a World Cup qualifier and won 2–1. Outside, I stopped at a kiosk to buy cigarettes. An old man, seventyish, stood there munching chocolate. "England?" he asked, beaming. I smiled and nodded. "Wembley! Puskás! Six-three!"

Right, I thought. Elbow on the counter, I fixed my face in his direction, then began. "Grosics, Buzánszky, Lorant ...." His approving smile faded into bewilderment, perhaps at my powers of recital, probably at the sternness of my delivery. "....Budai, Kocsis, Hidegkuti ...." I gave him them all. He gawped. I hadn't finished: merely paused. "Merrick, Ramsey, Eckersley ...." He muttered something to the vendor and turned to leave. "....Wright, Johnston, Dickinson ...." The face that looked round from his retreat belonged to someone escaping the clutches of a madman. "....Matthews, Taylor, Mortensen ...." He mustered a stride, not turning again. "....Sewell, Robb!"

The old boy – bless him – wasn't the only vanishing act that Hungary had seen. Three years earlier its government had removed the electrified fence on its Austrian border and thousands of East Germans seized the opportunity of fleeing to the West. But long before that, Hungary's prestige had vanished from the football world.

The overnight train from Prague had arrived in Keleti station two hours late at ten o'clock, but although it'd given me ample time to sleep off the previous evening's liquid excesses I was still in no mood for the hassle of seeking digs. Thankfully, these came to me on the concourse. She was wizened, slight of build, around sixty, and grabbed my left elbow to swing me round. "You want room? You come. Very nice." Her photocopied little cut-up spoke, in English, of a room to let in the centre, that last word emboldened, but it still took a taxi to reach it. The tatty door on the street looked insignificant amid the urban bustle, the rattling trams, the seething pavements, the tall, faceless, gapless blocks in need of a good sandblast. Opened, it revealed an amazing spaciousness beyond: here was a huge courtyard sprouting staircases and balconies. Somehow, the clicking heels and barked orders of Nazis became imaginable, people draped over these balconies to watch the urgent pandemonium of Jewish neighbours being long-ago dragged away. The ornate though murky tenement flat soon held mystery of a more immediate, audible nature. Having flopped onto the vast bed to reorientate myself, staring at the distant ceiling, I then became subjected to a full-volume airing of Napalm Death, and this pneumatic drill was definitely within. Mrs Horesnyi was evidently an old bat with an eccentric taste in musical companionship. The door ajar, it was a subsequently disappointing discovery to see a duly-fixed twenty-something son appear and quickly beat an exit. I was in no such rush myself. Fradi's game was a five o'clock kick-off: ample time to reacquaint myself with the air of a captivating city.

The hub of Hungary indeed – two million people, a fifth of the country's population, live here – Budapest's status as the centre of power, commerce and culture is transcended by its utter charm, one that is enhanced by a turbulent past and a curiosity of origin. The Magyar tribes were a migrant, Asiatic people who have provided a present-day idiosyncrasy among European language structures. Hungarians rightly claim that theirs ranks as one of the world's truly difficult tongues. But it's easy to stroll along the Pest bank of the Danube, look over to hilly, leafy Buda with its grand old architecture and spectacular medieval monuments – all the more romantic when bathed in illumination at night – and rejoice that a spirited people, repressed by Turks and Habsburgs, occupied by Nazi Germany and crushed by Soviet tanks, have kept their distinctive identity and their capital city both alive and dreamy.

Leaving for a while its smart boulevards, designer stores and chic cafés – "the Paris of Eastern Europe" – and its less salubrious drinking holes offering harsh wine by the cheap ladle-load amid the thick cigarette smoke and noisy eating of the city's more earthy characters, I caught the metro through Pest to Népliget station. I emerged onto the pavement of Üllői út, a wide expressway that nondescriptly cuts a concrete path towards Hungary's sole airport and enables speedy buses to be overtaken by even speedier traffic. This was the IX district of Budapest, the most working- class of the city's inner suburbs. Not far away stood the remnants of a barracks whose officers in 1956 had been the first to support the people in their ill-fated challenge to Moscow's suppression. Much nearer, immediately in view upon leaving the subway, was the home of Fradi: Ferencvárosi Torna Club, universally known as simply Ferencváros, the best supported and historically most successful football team in Hungary.

The first thing I noticed was that practically everyone had clothed themselves in Fradi's green and white. An attached bar that doubled as an unpretentious restaurant, whose tables spilled airily onto Üllői út, had attracted several elderly fans thus resplendent. Wherever I go, I love this: God keep them safe and ever hopeful in their loyalty for as long as they still live. (Sadly, a less heart-warming element has also attached itself to the club, its image afflicted by a serious hooligan problem. Ferencváros fans had been prominent in the brawling when England played at the Népstadion back in October 1983, whilst twelve years later the right-wing extremists among them would infamously aim racist chants at Ajax's several black players during a UEFA Champions League match.)

At forty pence a pint, prior to taking my eighty-five pence seat inside the stadium, I enjoyed a couple of beers under the canopy and reflected upon a previous visit when the price of another commodity had pushed the country, in the words of President Árpád Göncz, "to the brink of revolution". I'd intended, back in October 1990, to watch Honvéd play Szeged, but that match had been called off because Szeged had been unable to travel. Striking lorry and taxi drivers had blockaded roads for three days in protest at the government's doubling of petrol costs. As tensions escalated between the protesters and pro-government demonstrators, the new post-Communist régime faced a real crisis as it began grappling with painful economic reforms and the requirement to retain the confidence of foreign investors. The Prime Minister, József Antall, had needed to go on television to pacify the nation and admit that the plan to raise the price of petrol had been a blunder.

At least the lack of fare at Honvéd's small, undistinguished looking stadium had enabled me then to sample the altogether different home of another Hungarian legend. Whilst Honvéd had found renaissance during the 1980s, their true glory years had been three decades earlier as the team of the army, the Communist masters' favourite, the plundered nucleus of an entrancing national side. But their postponed game on that day had redirected me to possibly the most atmospheric football ground I've ever experienced anywhere, a setting positively reeking of history: from much earlier than Honvéd's heyday.

The sole covered stand had been rebuilt after World War Two but still somehow belonged to the youth of its majority of occupants, septuagenarians, and beyond. To my right was a clanking railway line and a belching chimney. Opposite was the back of an even more eerie, olde-worlde ground, lowly BKV Előre's, these the two closest stadia in Europe. The whole place seemed a smoky relic, evocative of a lost age and the players who'd once graced it as MTK, led by their president Alfred Brüll, became in the words of the renowned expert Willy Meisl, brother of Hugo, "the finest side in (Continental) Europe". Among those players had been icons: György Orth, a versatile genius considered by many the best Hungarian footballer of all time; the forward Alfred Schaffer, described by Willy Meisl as "of world class when barely sixteen"; Imre Schlosser, scorer of 59 goals in 68 appearances for Hungary, who caused an uproar when leaving Ferencváros for MTK during World War One. These men had starred as MTK – inspired for several seasons by Jimmy Hogan – won ten Championships in a row from 1914. In each of the four seasons previous to that, MTK had finished runners-up to Fradi. This was a rivalry from the mists.

But the MTK Stadion – also the club stage of one Nandor Hidegkuti – had other tales to tell. The club's Jewish links incurred the wrath of Nazi Germany, Brüll and others perishing in the gas chambers. The early 1950s saw the Communist rulers, typically, playing name games: for a while MTK were known as Vörös Lobogó (Red Banner) and were indeed the team of the ÁVO secret police, giving Honvéd a run for their money, too. There would follow forty-odd years of scant success though, before, as the nineties unfolded, takeover by the flourishing Fotex group would bring a new businesslike approach, rejuvenation, and a dramatic double in 1997. Thus have MTK Budapest somehow come to symbolise the grand old and just possibly the new of Hungarian football, certainly its trials and tribulations in between.

As for Fradi, on the domestic scene anyway, they'd never really gone away, despite having suffered more than most in the new post-Second World War political structure. The only Hungarian club to have won a European trophy, the Fairs Cup in 1965 by defeating Juventus in the final, the only one to have boasted a European Footballer Of The Year in Flórián Albert, and alone in never having been relegated since their formation in May 1899, Ferencváros had paid dearly for being the traditional focus of a right-wing neighbourhood. Indeed, they had been the favoured team of the Nazi Arrow Cross, a puppet government installed by the occupying Germans. Between 1951 and 1956, the era of the Stalinist dictator Mátyás Rákosi, they'd lost their historic name to be called Kinizsi after an ancient Magyar figure, and Honvéd had grabbed from them Budai, Kocsis and Czibor, three of the Wembley maestros. But the spirit of the club, twice Mitropa Cup winners between the wars, proved undying and

Üllői út, home of Fradi, scene of Hungary's greatest shame

by this first weekend of June 1992 they'd won the most league titles (23) and the most cups (15). Although they hadn't been Champions in any of the last ten seasons, today they were chasing hard number twenty-four.

Practically coverless, the 20,000-capacity ground was virtually full and throbbing with support: "Hoy-yah Fradi! Hoy-yah Fradi!" would come in loud unison from everywhere. That eighty-five pence seat unfortunately plonked me right on the front row close to a corner-flag, behind the wire mesh of tall caging, not the best view I've ever had. An unusual sight, just to my right in front of the modern clubhouse and a short pass away from the goalposts, was the stone statue of a naked man, a memorial to the club's founding father, Ferenc Springer.

He didn't need to spring to Fradi's defence now. In a match whose most memorable feature was the midfield space afforded its contestants – these players just wanted to play, not fight – Ferencváros looked the more likely side throughout, despite the most eye-catching performer being their young sweeper, András Telek, whose reading of the game was spot-on: a month earlier he'd played a part in Hungary's restricting England to a 1–0 win in a Budapest friendly. With a goal in each half, including a last-minute penalty, Fradi duly saw off their opponents Pécsi MSC; and with a tremendous run of fourteen wins and three draws in their closing seventeen matches, they would duly clinch the Championship a single point ahead of Vác FC Samsung.

As the crowd seeped away contentedly, the Üllői út stadium revealed its beloved colours in the form of the plastic seating mounted upon concrete. MTK this wasn't; but nor had it always been thus. Once, whilst much more commodious and atmospheric, it had been wooden – its character when England lost here 1–2 in 1934, and when later the scene of a terrifying crumble with the place packed for another international against Austria in May 1947. Twenty-odd years after that, Fradi would need to vacate it for five years while it was wholly renovated.

Not a process applied to Hungarian football itself. On the evening of Wednesday 29th October 1997, for a World Cup qualifier, a mere 13,175 folk would come to Üllői út and witness a nadir. With half an hour still to play, and Puskás reportedly reduced to tears in his seat, Yugoslavia were seven-nil up. A substitute called Illes pulled one back two minutes from the acrid end, as irrelevant to the crushing humiliation as it was to Hungary's plummeting down the FIFA world rankings. Just prior to that massacre, they'd stood 68th. Kuwait, Trinidad & Tobago, Gabon and Thailand were some of the nations above them. By March 1998 they were 82nd and trailed Togo.

Every nation has its spells in the doldrums, but Hungary's vessel represents a peculiar voyage indeed. For such a traditional battleship to virtually disappear from radar and remain inconsequential for so very long is a unique tale of decline that is as strange as it is sad.

Willy Meisl had spoken of their having done more than any other nation to raise Central European football to the standard of the British innovators as the infant game on the Continent developed. They raised themselves so well that they reached the World Cup Final of 1938, although Sárosi, Zsengellér and the rest were outpowered in Paris by Pozzo's Italy. By that time professionalism had been introduced. The shamateurism of post-WWII Communist rule would subsequently celebrate one of the finest teams ever to grace football, a generation of players brought together, similarly to the Dutch of 1974, as if by celestial decree. On 14th May 1950 Hungary lost 3–5 a friendly in Vienna. On 19th February 1956 they lost 1–3 another friendly in Istanbul. In between, they were defeated but once. Their team which won Olympic gold in 1952 was the one that soon provoked a radical, seminal rethinking of our own insular, complacent attitude (not least with regard to the value of coaching, previously viewed with disdain, and of international match preparation) as they foxed England with a brand of football hitherto unseen. It was our first defeat on home soil by foreign opposition, our notion of supremacy was shattered, it was the rudest of wide awakenings.

Billy Wright, England's captain on that fateful afternoon of 25th November 1953, said later that he, "sensed the astonishment of the Wembley crowd at the ball juggling and shooting of the Hungarians, while we were all kicking in before the game". Such artistry and power translated indeed into a match performance revered by its fortunate observers. They spoke of the Hungarians' sublime self-belief and comfort in possession, so that balls would be played even to those tightly marked; of their skill in outwitting and escaping opponents; of the mix of passes short or long; of unerring positional sense, mobility and interchangeability; of supreme physical fitness; of a tactical nous that embarrassed accepted stereotype. Árpád Csanádi, a contemporary Hungarian and "master-coach" author of a 700-page tome covering every aspect of preparation from "goalkeeper's defensive technique without the ball" to the nutritive content of "biscuit, twice toasted" (the book in question was entitled: *Soccer* ....), noted that the deep-lying centre-forward Hidegkuti and right-half József Bozsik were allowed at Wembley "to work practically unchallenged". It was a beautiful display that utterly flummoxed England because its concept was so completely alien to our own rigid convention. And the concept – useless, as is any theory, if not practicable – was enacted by masters. Like Ferenc Puskás. No wonder he could barely stomach Üllői út forty-four years on.

That one match, out of exactly fifty, which Hungary lost after Vienna – Sod's Law beyond its most dastardly – happened to be the 1954 World Cup Final against West Germany, 2–3, when a two-goal lead was thrown away. In an earlier group game, Hungary had buried the Germans 8–3. Unbelievable. So too is that such a thoroughbred footballing nation should slide into apathy. So how come?

The 1956 Uprising's backlash is no answer. For all that the "Magical Magyars" team thus broke up – some of the Honvéd club touring South America at the time of the rebellion decided not to return home, among them Czibor and Kocsis who subsequently joined Barcelona, while Puskás would eventually take out Spanish citizenship – later Hungarian national sides, though naturally pale in comparison, would emerge to resuscitate the esteem. World Cup quarter-finals were reached in 1962 and 1966; a 3–1 defeat of Brazil by a team featuring Bene and Albert, Farkas and Rákosi, would enrapture Goodison Park. The 1972 European Championships saw Hungary reach the semi-finals. Three successive World Cup qualifying campaigns would see them top their groups; the last of those, for 1986, involved a victory in Rotterdam against Rijkaard, Gullit, van Basten and company.

But that Finals tournament in Mexico brought not only, like the previous two, earliest exit, but also a thumping so catastrophic as to seemingly inflict some coma. In their opening group game Hungary lost 0–6, and to the despised USSR at that. For many fans, already dismissive in their comparison of the current standard and then scandalised by domestic match-fixing, something died in Irapuato. As for the national team itself, victories since that day have been almost invariably against mere third-rate teams or worse. Hungary haven't qualified for the World Cup Finals since, nor indeed for the European Championships since 1972. In 1994 they would play twelve matches and fail to win any, one of their eight defeats being 1–7 in Eindhoven. Their club sides make no impact in European competition and only one player, midfielder Lajos Détári, for whom Olympiakos of Greece actually paid Eintracht Frankfurt nearly five million pounds in July 1988, has had any real profile away from his homeland in recent years. Nor, in recent years, has any Hungarian coach emulated the likes of Benfica's Béla Guttmann of the early sixties, Spain's Ladislao Kubala of a decade later, or Puskás himself who took Panathinaikos to the 1971 European Cup Final. Hungary's national coach, meanwhile, has taken on the appearance of an annual appointment, and often a recall to office at that.

Two factors seem predominant in this slide: weak leadership, and dubious fibre below – a recipe that makes their plight perhaps not so surprising after all. Whilst the latest political upheaval adversely affected the game's financial support, the Hungarian FA has been seen for years as ineffectual, entirely lacking in dynamism and incapable of formulating a coherent strategy that would bring revival. And this lack of dynamism pervaded the game as a whole. After the defeat by Iceland just before my visit, the coach at that time, Emerich Jenei (a Romanian), lamented, "The mentality must be changed generally, and in the clubs. If they achieve something small they become too satisfied. You have to do more. It is no wonder that Hungarian clubs don't progress far in Europe. That is the strength of a country's football, and then the national team can benefit too." In the autumn of 1992 Puskás returned home and was appointed by the FA to a wide-ranging role that saw him cast as roving ambassador and responsible for the improvement of youth football. He soon replaced Jenei as national coach, and just as quickly relinquished the reins. In 1995, invited to Stan Matthews' 80th birthday bash, Puskás said, "I'll talk about anything, but don't ask me about Hungarian football."

Lack of improvement was underlined by the pithy comments of the then coach Janos Csank immediately after the mauling by Yugoslavia in October 1997, when he said that the nation's problems came from "upstairs". One of those mauled, Flórián Urban, was more trenchant: "When the FA officials don't do their job, what do you expect?" A year earlier Csank had already expressed his view that Hungarian football still needed to change substantially "at all levels". "More has to be done for youth development, more coaching in schools. Instead of a pyramid structure we've got the opposite, top-heavy with not enough going on at the base."

In outlining the problems in the aftermath of that Iceland match, Jenei had also aired a critique of the players themselves: "They are not strong enough physically. They are not tough enough as football personalities." Csank spoke similarly just prior to Hungary's 0–3 defeat at Wembley in May 1996. The mentality of Hungarian footballers had been called into question much earlier, though.

Back in 1968 an English FA staff coach had spent a month in Hungary widely studying their game, and his report contained some telling comments. " ....The work rate of the players was not very good at all ....they do not appear to fight when they get behind ....people continually stressed to me that the players were tired – they certainly looked tired, but I am certain that this tiredness was only a condition of the mind ....I felt that throughout Hungarian soccer there was a general lack of confidence .... personally, I feel that it is the attitude from the top which allows this air of undiscipline ...." Certain players came in for particular criticism. "When I watched Farkas in training he took it very easy and looked apparently disinterested. This was also reflected in the way he played. Albert confirmed what I had suspected through seeing him in the World Cup in England – that he is inconsistent and has a bad attitude." The English coach went on: "This attitude of the stars permeates throughout Hungarian soccer ....the young players obviously emulate the stars ...."

Hungary did make some attempt to address their problems during the 1970s, having realised that international football by then indeed required greater physical condition and combative spirit. In 1975 Lajos Baróti was reinstalled as national coach, steered them to the World Cup Finals three years later – Hungary had failed to qualify for the previous two – and he was satisfied that his players no longer feared physical contact. But in Argentina, Hungary lost all three of their group games, and just prior to that tournament they had been not only outwitted 1–4 by Ron Greenwood's England at Wembley but also overpowered. One player in that match embodied the entire Hungarian malady.

In June 1992 Tibor Nyilasi coached Ferencváros – whose vice-chairman was Flórián Albert – to their league title. Back on 24th May 1978, as a temperamental 23-year-old midfielder, he was considered the major star of both Fradi and his country. Though tall he was tricky and had twinkling feet, and he set up Hungary's goal with an outrageous dummy. But one moment in the first half spoke volumes. Having played an unbelievably sloppy ball when facing his own goal near the corner of the penalty-area, he then made not the slightest attempt to retrieve the dangerous situation he'd caused. In my notes on that game, I wrote: 'Nyilasi – superbly talented but slack, occasionally to the point of negligence'.

Nowadays, dismally, Hungary lacks such talent either on the pitch or off it, and is just negligent. The nation has failed to grasp football's changing times. Players of Nyilasi's capability, redolent of the archaic fifties, don't exist. Those fans still wistful of that goulash past are served up gruel. Fans more youthful are also being lost, the game of less interest than ever to a new generation. Several of those that are attracted to it seek violence. Not long after my visit, police shot two Fradi hooligans in the leg after a game at Újpesti, and when MTK won the Cup again in 1998 two hundred Újpesti fans invaded the pitch at the final whistle to threaten them. "Unfortunately," observed Csank, "football is not as popular as it used to be in Hungary."

Perhaps MTK's fresh policy will point the way. But perhaps Ferenc Puskás' heart will eventually break. One thing's for sure. I'll never sell his autograph.

There was some dubious selling in Budapest on the Saturday night of 6th June 1992, though. At just before eight o'clock I wandered inside a very smart, spacious bar, still in Pest, and was glad of some respite from the day's bustle, for the place was empty. My only company as I sat on a bar stool was a grossly overweight female to serve me, but although she kept disappearing, eventually three suited bouncers would also appear in the doorway. I leisurely drank four small glasses of beer and also bought a packet of cigarettes. The woman continually filled the nut bowl, which I assumed was a common courtesy. At this time the exchange rate was as little as 140 forint to the pound. When the bill came, she wanted 1,600 forint. Those nuts were quite pricey. As I complained, a youthful barman materialised too, and I noticed his very sheepish look. Slapping 600 forint on the bar, I said, "That's yer lot. I'm off." My disgust was heightened as I walked across the still deserted room by the opportunist fat bitch's cry of "asshole!" But I now realised I had to negotiate the goons. Amazingly, to a man, they were Farkas.

Beer prices varied wildly. Across the Chain Bridge in delightful Buda, a small glass of horse piss cost 215Ft in one bar, yet just around the corner in a comparable setting a large glass of tasty dark beer cost 88Ft.

Strolling back along József körút to Mrs Horesnyi's (Sunday's light would later reveal to a closer eye bullet holes on this road, poignant evidence that the area had indeed been a major theatre of the Uprising) I was propositioned at two in the morning by a pair of male transvestite, lipsticked hookers. József körút, with its topless bars and streetwalkers, was obviously at the bottom end of Pest's sex industry now. My own laughter in the night air with that of the harmlessly half-cut freaks alerted someone else on the lonely pavement. At first sight I wondered if it was somehow my landlady, improbably pursuing some mercy mission on my behalf, for she looked similar and the same age too. As she neared, with an unknown smile, I wondered further if this could be for real. "Come! I am girl!" Soon I saw her taken into a taxi by a punter in his twenties. Imagination revolted.

Apart from letting the Népstadion fill my mind for a time the following day, there were other sights and reflections to ponder. An enchanting ninety-minute evening cruise along the Danube provided a glide past the most significant structure: the vast Parliament building, its architectural mix nudging at the Pest embankment. Here decisions had been taken – encouraged by Gorbachev in his policy of rapprochement and refusal to interfere in any reformist intentions of Warsaw Pact nations – that would initiate the momentous dismantling of the Iron Curtain itself.

In early 1989 the ruling Communists of Hungary, which for years had enjoyed standards of living far beyond its cousins in the Soviet bloc, finally opted to act upon their (and Gorby's) recognition that the prevailing order was dying on its shelf. On May 2nd, risking trouble with those cousins, but to an invited gathering of Western television crews, Hungary symbolically cut the fence – maintained till then only for the convenience of others, since Hungarians already had freedom of movement – on its frontier with Austria. The pictures echoed far. The Lake Balaton region, perennially a popular holiday spot for East Germans – and now was the season – became particularly attractive. Just beyond Austria, West Germany's Basic Law made provision for all blood Germans: new passports would be available. Lake Balaton had never been so flooded, nor had a fence become so cluttered.

The process became inexorable. Naturally encouraged too by the politicians of the West – President Bush among them – and their promises of financial reward, Hungary went the whole way and officially opened the entire border on September 10th. The haemorrhage of bewildered East German refugees became accompanied by an upsurge on the streets of Dresden, especially Leipzig, and ultimately East Berlin, that not even Budapest had ever seen. Honecker's ploy of persuading Czechoslovakia to seal its border to prevent East Germans reaching Hungary merely resulted in hundreds of his prisoners already in Prague storming the friendly West German embassy there. Farce now took over. Honi's naive solution to his massive dilemma was a one-off arrangement.

He would submit to the wishes of those camping in Prague by delivering them indeed to West Germany, by special train, but these trains – obstinately – had to be routed via East Germany. Obstinacy was lost in sheer provocation. When the en-route citizens of Dresden got wind of this insufferable favour, the inevitable huge riot occurred at their railway station. Moreover, the West German embassy in Prague simply refilled. Meanwhile the GDR's Politbüro, appreciating the tide as protest swelled, was plotting behind Honecker's back. Having then wrested a power of sorts, their first futile gesture to the people was an introduction of freedom to travel. This concession they utterly cocked up; and East Germany's jail, so austere and so unbreachable for forty years, suddenly had countless Ronnie Biggs' lining up for the laundry wagons and ladders. Because of incohesion and misinterpretation among the new governors, a premature and erroneous announcement was broadcast on GDR television on the evening of November 9th. The instructionless border guards at the Berlin Wall, facing an immediate and impossible crush, finally lifted the barriers. The Wall crumbled. The world, whose recognition of his utopian entity Honecker had forever craved, now saw how orgasmic his former subjects were in being able to leave it.

The domino effect then toppled the Communist bloc as a whole. The Curtain let in daylight.

Hungary – the erstwhile "happiest hut in the camp" – will thus be enshrined, happily at last, in history. Whilst the refiguration of Eastern Europe would bring serious problems, not least those of nationalism and economic hardship, and Gorby would become vilified in his own homeland as at best some idealistic incompetent, many folk have Hungary to thank. For all its problems, what worth is life if you can't explore and don't have a voice? In 1989, Hungary showed its balls.

Pelé (1997): "Hungary has fallen out of love with football."

Széchenyi (1830): "Many people think that Hungary was; I like to believe that she will be!"

Count István Széchenyi, a philanthropic patriot, is widely regarded as 'the greatest Hungarian'. Many today will share his hopes so far as football's concerned. If only Hungary could show its balls there, too.

Chapter 11

Chorus of Disapproval

Italy: San Marino v England 17/11/93

One of football's more inglorious competitions it may have been, an artificial conception whose strange existence came to be barely acknowledged even by many of its participants, but it nevertheless brought about some delightful tours. One of these also took in an England game, conveniently just an hour's train ride away out of Tuscany and across the Appennines, when a fulminating rendition of arrivederci from travelling fans echoed around a ghostly stadium and left the man in no doubt that his passing was welcomed. It was somewhat ironic that he should take his leave here. Three and a half years earlier in this very stadium Bobby Robson's England had seen off Belgium to reach a World Cup quarter-final, and that team had indeed been capable of winning Italia '90. Despite such inheritance, the man had brought mean times in the meantime. Did he not fare well.

It was a fixture the night before Graham Taylor's ignominious exit in Bologna which had formed the real point of that particular trip to Italy in mid-November 1993. In honesty, it was all a bit sad, and very false, especially to veterans such as Mick and myself who'd once upon a time followed Albion abroad for ties that had carried real competitive meaning.

The Anglo-Italian Cup, in one of its previous lives, though then too a mere fun tournament as John Osborne might have labelled it, had at least carried some semblance of credibility. Its 1971 version had been contested by top-division clubs that had seen fit to field virtually their strongest line-ups: when Albion played Inter Milan they'd faced Facchetti, Mazzola and Boninsegna, whilst Luigi Riva had stepped out for Cagliari at The Hawthorns along with Albertosi and Domenghini. English newspapers had provided sizeable match reports, and when Swindon Town won the 1970 competition photographs had shown an almost full house in Naples. Torrential rain had been much blamed for keeping the attendance down to ten thousand on the evening we'd played in the San Siro. But when the competition was again resurrected in 1993, things were wholly different. Random selection of participants was now con-

The Ponte Vecchio looking scruffy and the Arno looking dirty

fined to second-division outfits, and Channel Four's front man in Italy had been unaware of our match in Florence.

We went for the craic, some to behold a legendary city, to fly the flag in a very appealing land, and to watch the Baggies exotically take on a team that, aside from having been twice champions of Italy, had also actually won a bona fide continental competition and faced di Stefano's Real Madrid for the prize of the 1957 European Cup, too. Earlier that year, while Fiorentina had wrestled with the cream of Serie A prior to their inconceivable relegation, we'd been tramping Field Mill and Millmoor. Such stark contrast had been underlined the very day prior to our setting out for the Stadio Comunale when we'd seen Albion dumped out of the FA Cup by non-league Halifax Town at the Shay Ground. So how would we fare now against Gabriel Batistuta and Stefan Effenberg? They weren't there: away on national duty. Even our lot left players out. The fixture's nonsense thus plumbed a depth lower still. Just over five thousand, three more than I'd envisaged, stomached an insipid affair which I spent watching the ghosts of Hamrin, Amarildo and Antognoni. At one point I saw Dragan Dzajic enter the floodlit night and volley Yugoslavia into the 1968 European Nations' Cup Final at the expense of Banks, Moore, Charlton and company. Throughout, I wondered if Albion could ever again graduate to real events in such arenas. We lost 0–2, and nobody gave a toss. Nobody had a kind word for our club's overseers, either. Their short official excursion had been highly unattractively priced and they'd announced that it would be impossible to buy match tickets through any other source, and therefore pointless travelling under your own steam. Having ignored such claptrap, and not wanting to be herded into £20 seats anyway, our lot walked into some cake shop upon arrival and a fat bloke behind the counter had saved us another twelve quid each. Thus we sat high opposite the main stand for an equally splendid view, and unmolested by the local *tifosi*.

One of the genuinely fine elements of those expeditions to Italy would indeed be the respectful and welcoming attitude of the residents, willingly reciprocated in West Bromwich. Folk bent over backwards in their appreciation of the few supporters who'd travelled so far for such a non-event out of devotion to their team. Where the Anglo-Italian Cup's concerned, this is my most abiding memory: even of Brescia, but especially of Salerno.

Hospitality in that pit of the Amalfi Coast's arm – Salerno is usually viewed as just that, unfairly out of comparison with the limb – pushed definition to its extreme. Having ridden from seedy, chaotic Naples, begetter of Caruso, pizza, luscious Loren and syphilis, and via Pompeii, a more celebrated victim of infection, we quickly set up camp outside a bar opposite Salerno's railway station on Corso Vittorio Emanuele, the city's smart main shopping drag. A giant Albion flag immediately adorned its exterior, a liberty that drew warm smiles from passers-by, came to magnetise other dribbling Baggies, and was heartily endorsed by the hosts, who readily entered into our spirit and would regularly feed it with plates on the house. It was here that Vincenzo would eventually happen by and draw up a chair.

Stout, in his late fifties, he would have been most mothers'-in-law worst nightmare: but many male drinkers' dream company, and not just because he absolutely insisted on paying, an early illustration of the generosity we'd experience here. His excellent English had been honed during his erstwhile days as a club owner in Soho. He was sexist, devil-may-care, had survived his own roguishness, seen the world in both its geographical and human contexts, topped up his funds nowadays through "buying and selling", and sat there jovially replete in his winking, philosophy-sussed comfort. I also counted four well-dressed women – typically, in this country, photogenic – greet him along their way. What had brought him back to Italy? "It became impossible any more to remain a step ahead." When he came back from the toilet he immediately began talking about football instead. He laughed that, aside from Arsenal's being his favourite team, Salernitana were crap. I didn't probe this either, even though I felt he was now risking arrogance despoiling this amiably larger-than-life profile and, from what little I knew of the local club, that he was being a little unfair.

Salernitana, who'd recently moved from their aged 12,000-capacity home into a new stadium where 40,000 had crammed to see the national team beat Estonia in a Euro '96 qualifier six months earlier, had indeed won nothing over the course of their 76-year history. But the previous season they'd been denied a first ever ascent to Serie A only by a last-gasp defeat and their home attendances had averaged twenty thousand, an unusually healthy gathering for the second division. This level of support, and that spitefulness of fate, touched a recognisable chord. Perhaps because this was merely the Anglo-Italian Cup and thus devoid of severity, perhaps because our fiftyish-few invasion obviously wanted only to party, and just possibly because some of the locals had read that our club, however proud, was looked upon as some afterthought too, there was chemistry. This bubbled nowhere better than in the moments prior to kick-off.

In their wisdom the police decided to institute divorce proceedings. A shared, harmonious gathering in the steep upper tier at one end of the roofless concrete now saw home supporters allowed to keep that abode but Albion fans banished to the lower tier. As sticks pointed the way to segregation, the Salerno folk howled their derision: at the police. Our lot departed to honest applause. A dozen *carabinieri* caravans and six ambulances were meanwhile parked outside. Had these police been English batsmen their averages would have been phenomenal. Or would they? Not long into the goalless game, the Campanian night air became a fireworks display and the upper tier a bathroom, the rain as violent as I've ever seen, and everyone remarried. The reason why at least one English newspaper estimated our following to be three hundred-strong was that 250 attentive locals enthusiastically joined in with 'Shit On The Villa'.

I looked out for Salernitana's progress afterwards. They went within another whisker of promotion that season but two years later would finally crack it after half a century, and then we saw how fervent their fans really were, if dubious in their behaviour. In November 1998 they got Fiorentina thrown out of Europe when a firebomb was chucked from the Arechi's stands as the players left the pitch at half-time, Fiorentina having been obliged to play their UEFA Cup-tie against Grasshoppers in Salerno because of previous misdemeanours of their own. The firebomb injured the fourth official and caused abandonment: a Salernitana fan had recently been stabbed in Florence, and here was revenge. Two months later they stormed a press conference in full view of television cameras, chairs flying, to demand their president's reinstating the sacked coach: and got their wish. In February 1999 Channel Four's coverage of their home fixture against Fiorentina showed a full house boiling over, a far cry from the three thousand who'd watched their reserves play Albion. Salernitana's valiant struggle to avoid immediate demotion, ironically ignited by replacement of that favoured coach, Delio Rossi, after all, would ultimately fail on the very last day. When a special train back from that heartbreak in Piacenza neared a tunnel on the approach to Salerno, some fans chose the wrong moment to light a smoke bomb. Four died in the fanned inferno.

We'd encountered no such doomed idiocy. While some of us moved along the coastline after our game, others were happy to remain. When I met up again with Mick at the airport on the Friday evening, he told me that he and two others had just spent a couple of days drinking beer and wine and eating pizza, mostly the treat of locals, who eventually drove them all the way to Naples and gave them a tour of that city too. Excessive natures can also do extraordinary good.

Those who prefer spick-and-span comfort would most likely not give Salerno a second look. Although a little on the scruffy side and pale compared with nearby true beauty spots – Amalfi, Sorrento, Capri – I loved it for its earthiness, warmth and total lack of pretentiousness. The British X Corps, who helped gain a beachhead here as part of the US Fifth Army in September 1943, wouldn't have scanned their surroundings for anything but enemy fire. Fifty-two years later, because of them, I was able to stroll that shoreline at dusk and have my eyes drawn to the brooding mountains in nothing but imagination. I don't equate enrichment with comfort. Only feelings count when you bow out.

The Amalfi Coast, though, was certainly special to the eye. I thought tiny Amalfi itself, most of which had been consigned to the Mediterranean by a fourteenth-century earthquake, looked divine in this early September heatwave as it nestled at the foot of spectacularly craggy mountains. But as for the Bay of Naples' jewel, Capri, it was predictably beset by even more fellow-grockles than cosy, cliff-top Sorrento, where at least I'd left the HP sauce bottle untouched as it stood on a pavement table, since my stomach likes to explore with the rest of me. Three years later Costantino Federico, Capri's mayor, would threaten to close its main port between ten and six in the evening to stop "invasions of daytripping barbarians who have no sense of style, leave lots of rubbish, and spend little money". Well, he can't have it all ways. Openly invited to delight in its heavenly spectacle, the visiting hordes have been screwed on Capri for years. Federico, while he would have been pleased that I dropped no litter, couldn't have been surprised at my refusal to spend more than three quid when all this bought was a tiny glass of Martini. And as I soaked up the views amid the idling crush, I also reflected upon the fact that Alfredo di Stefano's grandad had been forced to leave here for Buenos Aires, an indication that the island's lifeline had indeed been tourism.

Naples, defiant of looming Vesuvius and the rest of barely believing Italy if not the world itself, poverty-stricken, air-polluted, where the sole code observed (a highway one, like the law, doesn't exist) is *omertà*, the city in the hands of the Camorra, must be not only a teeming paradise for anarchists but also the ideal place on earth to hone your cuteness, which you'd need to do if aiming to spend time amid such squalid mischief. John Ruskin once described Naples as "the most loathsome nest of human caterpillars". It suited Diego Maradona so much that he spent seven years there as a folk hero. I spent just the one night. And had my sunglasses nicked in the Piazza Garibaldi the next morning.

I'd been warned about Brescia, too.

If that Salernitana game had been whirled and drenched by a squall, then the one in Lombardy three months later was not so much beset by the weather as wholly ridiculed by it. The Stadio Mario Rigamonti, where the great Hagi had once plied his trade, provided the biggest nonsense I'd ever seen in thirty-six years of watching football. The whole eerie place, virtually deserted, was suffocated by snow that filled the night air still. "Serata glaciale" was one of *La Gazzetta dello Sport*'s pithy descriptions, "impossibili condizioni" its terse summary. When Bob Taylor defied "equilibrio problematico" to dig out a late lone goal the ball doubled in size as it laboured across the cake, its final heap provoking a celebratory and suitably bizarre snowball fight between visiting players and fans. Thus indeed did this utter farce wholly ridicule the Anglo-Italian Cup itself, its fixture out of the way come what may, like unblocking the toilet.

Those 150-odd fans, confirmed by *La Gazzetta* as outnumbering Brescia's, included a few naughty, clever bastards who'd evidently taken in the previous Sunday's Milan-Napoli match and acquired there a native ditty which they reproduced now. "Go shove your prick up your own arse" was a rough translation. Unwise, as well as ungracious. Across the mesh, those few natives turned paroxysmal. At the final whistle, too, they gathered outside, where on a previous occasion they'd attacked Notts County supporters and bricked their bus. A Salernitana fan had mimed how knives in Brescia were used for other than spreading margarine and also told how drugs weren't always bought there over the counter. I didn't mind that the *carabinieri* held us all back for ten minutes and then provided an armed escort in the home of the Beretta towards the city centre, which unsurprisingly, thankfully, was deserted. Not the Solferino restaurant-bar, though.

Thirty of us had sought refuge there from the blizzard beforehand but found much more: the middle-aged host, Giorgio, was an absolute star. From the very first moment, as an endless conga of soiled and shivering navy blue and white crossed his threshold and sat down at his perfectly laundered cloths bedecking sturdily stylish tables, he'd opened the arms of his well-cut suit. Yes, of course, we were good for business on such an Arctic day, but this was well beyond that. Pizza on the house; engaging us all in beaming conversation by group. Now, till gone one in the morning, it was just the same, except that Mrs Giorgio turned her hand in the kitchen to free fare of a more recuperative substance, a massive urn of spaghetti to ladle into. On the assumption that this funny little competition had any reason behind it at all, and that being to foster Anglo-Italian relations, the Solferino was Wembley and Giorgio presented the Cup.

Why so many Albion fans making the haul? Bewitching, timeless, soothing Venice ("too much wairter" said Mick, his tongue bruising his cheek); sophisticated, businesslike Milan (where an evening's brandies session along Via Melchiorre Gioia came across "Luigi's little chicken": the great Riva's brother playing cards with the barman); the lakes (Stendhal had thought its turquoise waters and Alpine views made Como the most glorious spot on earth) .....

And so to the birthplace of the Renaissance. I occasionally wonder how some folk can fail to be captivated by football but I respect their preferences and leave them to it. I myself am unmoved by paintings, and I simply wasn't going to stand before Michelangelo or da Vinci so I could tick off their works for the expected sake of it. I also saw that, despite the sunshine, the Arno was dirty brown, and thought the Ponte Vecchio looked scruffy. I got more kicks from knowing that Dante, Galileo and Machiavelli had once walked here, and certainly from beholding Pisa's phenomenon an hour's train ride away. Whilst Venice is an entire dream – admittedly, my time there had been in December, uncrushed and without the stink – Florence has some buildings to visit. In between those buildings, the city now was badly congested by both humans and machines, often litter-strewn, and I eyed every moped with suspicion (one female Albion supporter predictably donated her handbag, one bloke was relieved of his wallet, another of a 100,000 lire note). I paid to enter the Duomo and climbed its 464 steps to an interior point wherefrom, for a marvellous view outside, I was first required to skirt a lengthily circular route whose safety barrier just survived my left knee. My fear of heights had worsened over the years – Cologne had been an early triumph – so that was that.

There were no Giorgios in Florence. Expectedly so, because restaurateurs there know that visitors form a mere turnover. One evening several of us found ourselves inside a large restaurant whose clientele was predominantly American, guidebooks and cameras readily visible, their swapped travellers' tales all too audible. The Black Country's finest, unimpressed, eventually provided an impromptu racket of their own. "Oh Andy Hunt! Is good up front!" arose the aria, saints marching in. "Oh Andy Hunt is good up front! 'E's gorra nairm that rhoymes with fanny, oh Andy Hunt is good up front!" As John-Boys awoke rubbing their eyes, Homers frowned beneath their baseball caps. Who were these Philistines in this nice liddle ol' home of Botticelli? "Whoa!" came a salacious response to the glowering of one Billie-Jean in particular. "Fancy bostin' a custard, darlin'?" But who were the bigger cliché?

It was strongly rumoured that, aside from Gabriel and Stefan, nor would employees of the Ferrovie Italiane dello Stato play ball either, to carry us into Bologna on the Wednesday afternoon. "Go an' make sure, Rich," said Great Barr estate agent Paul. I'd wondered if either Bill, a VAT-man of Five Ways, or Mick, might want to join in seeking confirmation. "Just go an' ask somebody in there." When I subsequently found them along the duly working train, a vast flagon of white wine bestrode the table: cheap enough not to learn till long afterwards that my share of its cost was actually the whole price. In Bologna, such cuteness would be of benefit to all.

The station there, where eighty-five had been slaughtered thirteen years earlier by a right-wing extremists' bomb in this historical heartland of Italy's lefties (the epithet of 'Red Bologna', though, could equally celebrate the handsome, prosperous city's strangely pervasive hue), was thick with England fans. These were mainly of a younger, disrespectful variety. When police were called, we four knew it was time to slope from the bar for self-determination to prevail.

Coming away, separately, from a kiosk behind one end of the stadium (our £3.50 tickets saved another fourteen quid), we were prepared for the inevitable, but still were amazed by the ease.

"Inghilterra?" confronted a cluster of uniforms.

"Americano," said I as Mick smiled benignly.

Two minutes later, Paul and Bill would emerge from a clump of trees as Irishmen. Bill part-was anyway, like most of Birmingham it seems.

Reunited inside that end of the mostly uncovered Renato dall'Ara, we found ourselves in the sole company of half a dozen San Marino supporters, whose flag Paul typically helped fly. Away to our left, beneath a strange red-brick tower from where Mussolini had rallied his blackshirts, a phalanx of Englishmen was meanwhile sealed by firepower. England's game here was practically a futile exercise even before it kicked off – Holland's scent of USA '94 at our expense was never going to be dulled by Poland the same evening – but I had other things on my mind.

What on earth had befallen Bologna? To this day their performance in cutting Albion to pieces in the old Inter-Cities Fairs Cup back in March 1967 remains one of my more memorable Hawthorns experiences: the team of Giacomo Bulgarelli, Helmut Haller and the lethal, quick-witted Dane, Harald Nielsen, who'd been Serie A's top scorer three years earlier when Bologna had won their seventh Italian championship. Even now, only Milan, Juve and Inter can boast more titles. That one in 1964 had been Bologna's last, though, and much worse had happened since. As I cast my eye over the largely deserted, historic splendour, spirits of the past seemed to wail feebly at the floodlit intrusion, for the place was a virtual graveyard, flowers laid every other weekend on Serie C matchdays. Nor was this predicament new: the club had descended into the third division during the eighties, managed to claw back to the first, but subsequently sunk all the way back again. Such catastrophe repeating itself, the tragedy seemed final, and once-mighty Bologna – twice Mitropa Cup winners, too – were staring dying-eyed at bankruptcy and, indeed, burial.

How could I have known then that a new president, Giuseppe Frascara, was heroically about to mastermind a marvellous, heart-warming redemption, which would see Bologna quickly reclaim their true status and even go desperately close to the UEFA Cup Final of 1999?

And how could I have known that, in the time it took me to put away my camera now, England's strange opponents – a motley crew of students, builders and coach drivers, and whose stamp-dealer manager had arrived at Heathrow back in February with a suitcase that burst open – would ludicrously steal in behind my back? Fiddling with a zip, I'd heard Paul – a veteran of Mexico '86 among other treks – laughingly exclaim, "Oh shit, they've scored!" Stuart Pearce's underhit backpass had invited Gualtieri after just nine seconds to notch only a third goal in their nineteenth match since FIFA's surprising admission of San Marino, a curious place of just forty square miles and 24,000 inhabitants, but the world's oldest as well as smallest independent republic. Any hopes, in taking this final World Cup qualifier from their tiny Serravalle home to the dall'Ara, that the attendance figure might approach that of their population, were indeed dashed though: 2,378 represented a record low for a match involving England.

They saw our red shirts duly recover to win in a canter, 7–1; but the Dutch meanwhile triumphed in Poznan and would accompany Norway to the Finals, with England going nowhere. Just as most of us had felt throughout Taylor's tenure.

If his replacing Bobby Robson had been an open secret, so too was his departure now. Towards the end of the game, those ranks of England fans gave their verdict. This region of Italy, Emilia-Romagna, had spawned the likes of Ferrari and Lamborghini, Mussolini and the film-maker Fellini: and Pavarotti. There were no tenors tonight. The clamour was even more rustic than the performance of the man's team here or in any other place.

"Fuck Off Taylor!!! Fuck Off Taylor!!! Fuck Off Taylor!!!"..... Six days later he resigned before being pushed.

You'd have to be a vegetable yourself not to have felt pleased for him on the Spring Bank Holiday Monday of 1999 when, in his second spell as their manager, he led Watford to an unlikely play-off victory at Wembley to earn a second successive promotion and a dreamy place in the Premiership. For one who'd been so pilloried – like no other manager in this country, by public and press alike – to subsequently produce such a fantastic achievement is inspirational to all.

The England job, though, had palpably been beyond him. Undoubted wholeheartedness – I'd once seen him, bathed in sweat, jogging along Birmingham's Broad Street at eight o'clock one morning – and geniality may assist towards getting blood out of stones at club level, inspiring unsung players into an unselfish determination not to be outdone, forging teams where the uncomplicated whole exceeds the sum of components. But polishing the national jewellery into a glitter that dazzles the smartest of opponents calls for more acute qualities: wit, tactical nous, and, before anything else, having the true respect of your well-prepared charges. This is how Venables was loved by the fans. They didn't give a toss about his off-field activities, nor that the media sucked up to him; what mattered was that he sent England players out onto the pitch comfortable in the knowledge that they were being guided by a real expert in whom they had utter faith, to whom they warmed, and thereby feeling capable of outdoing any opposition in such circles. If anyone might have come to emulate Sir Alf, it was Venables, and losing him must surely rank as one of English football's biggest mistakes.

A famous Channel Four documentary that charted Graham Taylor's demise sadly showed him lacking authority, suspiciously short of respect and, frankly, giving instructions whose vagueness would have had Sunday morning players sniggering in the pub toilet afterwards. Whilst his record as England manager over thirty-eight games would have accumulated sixty-seven league points, the real points were that we limped our way into Euro '92, failed to win any match having arrived there, then finished third of a group attempting to reach USA '94; and very often England looked wholly unrefined and ineffectual.

In between Robson's glorious failure of 1990 and Venables' of 1996 was a period best forgotten entirely. Our San Marino friends had even joined in the chorus.

Chapter 12
One Flag

Germany: Magdeburg v Bordeaux 23/10/90 & Dynamo Dresden v Malmö 24/10/90

On the evening of Wednesday 31st October 1990, four weeks after the country's political reunification, Germany played Luxembourg in a European Championship qualifier, winning by a surprisingly narrow margin of 3–2. It seemed strange, this first time, to see in the results section the formidable World Champions' name shorn of its prefix. It may have seemed surprisingly strange, also, for those who believed only English fans exported violence, to read that some Germans had been turned back at the border for carrying weapons, and that some who did make it to the newly upgraded Municipal Stadium had proceeded to destroy its plastic seats, hurl bottles, fight locals, demolish a food kiosk, then run riot afterwards through the cowering streets of the pleasant little Grand Duchy, resulting in thirty arrests. Deutschland einig Vaterland. Chancellor Kohl, figuring that to be seen emulating Bismarck wouldn't go amiss in the run-up to forthcoming elections, had speeded up the unification process. German thugs had lost no time, either: Luxembourg provided an early opportunity at a football match to be seen emphasising this status reclaimed after almost half a century.

Eight years on, despite their not having dared to offend at Euro '96 on the territory of their role models, an infinitely more fiendish attack would isolate a gendarme in a Lens sidestreet and leave him in a coma, prompting a local police spokesman to observe, "We do not believe English supporters are comparable to German hooligans. They do not have the same nasty streak."

My experiences in eastern Germany in October 1990 caused me not to be surprised in the slightest by the Luxembourg offensive a week later. And the calculated battering of Daniel Nivel in June 1998 was a darkly sinister outrage waiting to happen.

To be a young male living in Saxony or Saxony-Anhalt a year after the collapse of the Berlin Wall held mixed fortunes. Whilst the West, which formerly had been accessible only in wild dreams, was now open and alluring, eastern Germany was quickly becoming beset by a different reality. Kohl had promised its people "blossoming landscapes", but many gardens were already anything but rosy. Erich Honecker's Communist régime had provided full employment, with around eighty per cent of the workforce in State industries, mainly manufacturing. In the new market place, the inevitable would happen, and by late October 1990 a million eastern Germans were jobless. In the bleak apartment blocks of Magdeburg, prospects were even uglier than surroundings.

Nine-tenths of Magdeburg, the capital of Saxony-Anhalt, had been devastated by an Allied aerial assault in January 1945, and when the GDR set about reconstructing it taste was off the agenda as they seized upon uniformity. In June 1991, en route to Poland, I would awake on the autobahn, look from the coach window away to my right, guess immediately where I was, and have it confirmed. A sprawl of dehumanising concrete, where grim would be a charitable adjective, and emblem a suitable noun. Eight months before that, in the bowels of the place, I sensed that Magdeburg had been as much physically desecrated by its rebuilding as by its earlier bombing, for it looked to deserve better. Opera had ever been on its agenda, was still, whilst a river – the Elbe – always lends itself to tranquillity and a development of satisfactory ambience. The Elbe seemed tearful.

Into the new climate, nevertheless, had landed some colour in the form of huge, seductive department stores selling goods till now untouchable. While tiny groups of remaining 'guest-worker' Vietnamese peddled ghetto-blasters on opposite pavements, more substantial merchandise was now on offer. The Bonn government had decided to introduce parity where the Deutschmark and Ostmark were concerned: this arrangement had enabled Ossis to buy Wessi consumer goods – but, in ruining at a stroke eastern Germany's erstwhile low wage-cost structure, would jeopardise much further the region's attractiveness to business investors ...

For myself, the most symbolic development was to be found within the railway station. Magdeburg had formerly been so sensitive a location to the Soviets, a mere thirty miles from the Curtain, that they'd maintained their own strong presence here to reinforce the bulwark. Now, there was a passport photo-booth on the concourse. People today were being invited to please themselves. Among those, bereft of State support, who suddenly had to learn to fend for themselves, would be the football clubs of the former GDR.

Having eventually found somewhere – staid – to drink, I then left the central area for a twenty-minute stroll over and alongside the Elbe, past welcome parkland, to the Ernst-Grube-Stadion. Though barely noticed elsewhere, this would be a sadly historic night for 1.FC Magdeburg. The only GDR team to have actually won a major continental trophy, the Cup Winners' Cup in 1974 when they defeated no less than AC Milan in the final, they would surely never stage a European tie again. Cash-strapped oblivion awaited the former club of Martin Hoffmann, Jürgen Sparwasser and Joachim Streich in the coming new league structure.

The stadium itself was an appropriately sombre place. The floodlights, leaning to focus on the pitch, were as four torches whose batteries had run down. The mostly open terracing, holding 32,000 but only a fifth full, thus seemed shadowy bordering upon eerie. As for the match, a UEFA Cup second round first-leg, there would be much incident both on the pitch and off it. Especially the latter.

Magdeburg's opponents were not without their problems, either. Initially hailed as an entrepreneurial visionary, Claude Bez would be unmasked as a president so corrupt as to be eventually jailed. Bordeaux were currently twenty million pounds in debt and for that would be demoted at the end of this season to the French second division. At least they would bounce back and re-build. Tonight, their team contained a luminary or six: Lizarazu, Deschamps and Dugarry would be visited by glory eight years later; Kieft, the tall centre-forward, had been part of the Dutch European Champions' squad two years earlier; Patrick Battiston had been infamously flattened by Toni Schumacher during a 1982 World Cup semi-final; Joseph-Antoine Bell, from Cameroon, was a goalkeeper of repute. For Bell, this match would take its toll. It was a match that Bordeaux, despite Dugarry's sending-off on the hour by a hugely inept Austrian referee and their being pressured for much of the game (a certain Uwe Rösler, later of Manchester City, was prominent), won courtesy of a penalty-kick by Jean-Marc Ferreri in the last minute of the first half. The time-wasting and injury-feigning antics of the French didn't endear any onlooker. Several people present, however, needed no such excuse.

There was a pocket of around fifty Bordeaux supporters seated in block FIII towards the top of a bank overlooking the halfway line, just to my right. As soon as the game began, trickles of Magdeburg yobs wormed their way past me in ever-increasing numbers towards that pocket: some were skinheads, some wore the shirt of West Germany, some looked idiotic, many looked vicious. There they congregated. Apart from persistently monkey-baiting Bell, they spent the entire match taunting the French fans. Beer cans, too, would be hurled towards the pitch if a German player collapsed under a tackle or a linesman gave an unfavourable decision, and firecrackers were despatched onto the field without a damn for where they might land. Eventually, the tannoy broadcast warnings. At the final whistle there was a mob of fiendish intent loitering around block FIII. The police, who'd done absolutely nothing to apprehend the can-chuckers or dissolve the menace, now tightly enveloped the French while colleagues gently attempted persuading the thugs to disperse. I walked behind all of this in leaving the stadium, saw raw fear, and kept my mouth firmly shut. The following night would be a lot worse still.

It was a largely monotonous landscape that the morning train trundled through on its way from Magdeburg to Dresden, the only interest being the significance of those places it called at: Halle, birthplace of Händel; Leipzig, birthplace of Wagner, and the scene of massive street demonstrations a year earlier that pushed the teetering GDR ever closer to the brink. Dresden itself, capital of Saxony, the most densely populated area of eastern Germany, had two claims to pulchritudinal fame, one that still endured but the other savagely addressed by Bomber Harris in February 1945. Saxon women, like those of my home town Nottingham, are renowned for their allure; but the former so-called 'Florence Of The North', its baroque architecture by the Elbe celebrated by Canaletto two centuries earlier, had been firebombed, as an act of war debatable in the purest sense of that word, but as an act of desecration very sad. The Communists had chosen to leave some of the disfigurement – particularly the rubbled Frauenkirche (Church of Our Lady) – as an emblem of the West's dastardliness, and, as in Magdeburg, had rebuilt using concrete and steel. But there was still olde splendour, marvellous carvings, to enrich the eye, if not many bars to satisfy the throat.

At around six o'clock, two hours before kick-off, I made my way back to the Hotel Newa, a stone's throw on Leningrader Strasse from the main railway station. "Deutschland Hooligans! Deutschland Hooligans!" filled the early evening air. A hundred local youths had discovered that my digs were also housing Swedish visitors, and had formed a herd outside. Again, several shirts of West Germany were prominent. "Schwedische Schweinhunde!" I noticed that among the police who would eventually coax away these frothing beasts, many were smiling. The concierge wasn't as he finally let me through the door.

1.FC Dynamo Dresden's stadium had itself caught the fury of the Allied strike, and been rebuilt in quite extraordinarily shallow form. Nevertheless – smarter than Magdeburg's, with fresh-looking green and white predominant – the open Rudolf-Harbig-Stadion accommodated 38,000 and had regularly been over half-full during the days of the GDR, twice the national average. This support, despite the Dynamo label, reflected the footballing tradition of the club and the city. It was in Dresden, back in 1890, that an outfit called the English FC became the first in Germany to play according to the official Laws of the Game, and the old club itself, in its various guises over the years, had been prominent. The legendary Jimmy Hogan had coached between the wars Dresdner Sport-Club, a former long-serving player of which had been Helmut Schön, whilst no team would win more East German trophies than Dynamo Dresden. In this, the historic last season where such silverware was up for grabs, Dresden would finish runners-up in the table to Hansa Rostock and thus join them in entering the Bundesliga. There they would survive four seasons before finishing bottom beset by huge financial problems, and would quickly be consigned to regional amateur football, having been refused a trading licence amid an accounting scandal. Shame of another sort was much nearer. They would negotiate this European Cup second round, but not the next.

Denudation had already begun. Five players had recently been lost to western German clubs, among them Ulf Kirsten to Bayer Leverkusen and Matthias Sammer to VfB Stuttgart. Their opponents tonight, Malmö FF, were also acquainted with such inevitability, their admired youth system constantly producing talent that would emigrate: their team photograph in the match programme showed Roland Nilsson, Martin Dahlin, Stefan Schwarz and Patrik Andersson, but only the latter turned out here. So, too, did merely 6,870 people to watch, a surprisingly low attendance for all that the game, as had been Magdeburg's, was live on television. It was a match played largely in a fair spirit. Malmö – managed by Englishman Bob Houghton in his second spell with the club, his first having produced a European Cup Final appearance back in 1979 – looked the more accomplished side throughout, despite their adventurous first-half performance being quelled after the break by a Dresden team that huffed and puffed without effect. The Swedes' 18th-minute lead, a header by Leif Engqvist, was cancelled a minute from half-time, and the scorer would soon earn notoriety for erstwhile activity of a rather different nature. Sammer, whose father Klaus had suffered persecution and eventually dismissal from his job as Dresden's coach, would confirm that information about himself had been passed to the Stasi by former schoolmate Torsten Gütschow (and by another current Dynamo player, Frank Lieberam, whom he'd considered a close friend). Gütschow was the first footballer from the former GDR to own up to having been an informer, but also claimed that others at the club had in turn spied upon himself. This had been the price paid by many East German sportsmen for their privileges: grassing on their associates as the Stasi smelled State enemies everywhere. Some society.

If the spirit on the pitch was wholesome enough, things were wholly different off it. I was in block C, midway between halfway line and corner flag, and had a close view of what happened since the small group of Swedes – also numbering around fifty – sat immediately to my left. At the kick-off, thirty-odd

Dresden yobs moved to assemble within insult distance, directly in front of me. The Malmö fans were protected by nothing more than a couple of handfuls of stewards. As the match progressed, and particularly during the second half, certain members of this growing mob – who continued paying scant attention to the game – would attempt to slip through the flimsy cordon. At one point the Swedish flag was snatched and hauled away, dutifully retrieved by a brave steward. Once more, the police stood idly by. Just why the police (and that morning's *Der Magdeburger* newspaper had featured a piece bemoaning their worrying lack of presence) should have been so inert, and not fetched these troublemakers – and at least one thief – out of it, was beyond me: unless it had been GDR policy to tolerate up to a point rowdy behaviour as a means of allowing the youth population to let off a little steam now and again.

Eventually, though, the stewards became assailed by a concerted attempt, on the part of a by now sizeable mob of around eighty, to really physically get at the Swedes. A hail of beer cans, some of which again were also tossed onto the pitch, was followed by a flare arrowed right into their pen, for Christ's sake. With terror in the air, it was only then that riot police moved in wielding truncheons.

At the final whistle, booming chants of "Schwedische Schweinhunde!" from a lingering mob attracted dozens more from other parts of the ground, and these came running to add their presence. As I was leaving I turned to look again and saw the pocket of Malmö fans, as the French had been, almost hermetically sealed by a ring of uniforms, like some miniature GDR. Finding one set of gates locked, with another throng of around fifty Dresden louts gathered outside it, I walked on to another exit, this side of which the Swedes' team and supporters coaches were .parked. In the road a thick line of helmeted, batons-drawn police were holding at bay, but not charging, yet another steaming horde of around a hundred. This was raw, xenophobic evil, and when I eventually made my exit I took care to skirt the action, look as nonchalant as I could, and use the lamplight. With English clubs having just been readmitted to European competition after the post-Heysel ban, I also wondered what might have been the consequences had it been some of our lot instead of Malmö, and acting at least in self-defence before the police finally intervened. We'd surely have been blamed in the media. The *Daily Mail* could have had a field day. Integrity on the part of the official UEFA observer would have been sorely needed.

The events in Luxembourg the following Wednesday were predictable. As for Dynamo Dresden themselves, having eliminated Malmö on penalties, they would next face Red Star Belgrade in the March quarter-finals. Hammered 0–3 in Yugoslavia, they were trailing 1–2 in the second leg when their fans rioted with eight minutes left and the game was abandoned. Their subsequent two-year ban from Europe was immaterial. But the chords struck inside me by what I witnessed in Magdeburg and Dresden would echo.

Hooliganism was not exactly new to eastern Germany in 1990. Eleven years earlier we'd been warned to watch out for Carl Zeiss Jena's element, although nothing happened to us. It wasn't unheard of in western Germany either, for that matter. Despite rantings to the contrary by Colin Moynihan, the British Minister for Sport, German hooligans had been heavily prominent during Euro '88. Herbert Schnoor, state interior minister for North Rhine-Westphalia, declared that Germans, not the English, had provoked the serious disturbances when England played Holland in Düsseldorf. German police stated that most of the fighting during the first week of that tournament had been instigated by Germans or Dutch wanting to show they were harder than the English, and the majority of those arrested were German. Two years later, the then FIFA General Secretary Sepp Blatter would express surprise at finding that German fans had misbehaved during the World Cup Finals in Italy.

Domestic football in western Germany, however, had been largely unblighted, although there had been incidents: on the day of the 1982 Cup Final, for example, Frankfurt police had to water-cannon fighting fans of Bayern Munich and Nuremberg and subsequent rampages led to ninety-two arrests and over a hundred injured. With the country reunified, though, any outbreaks in the east were no longer subjected to news suppression, and towards the end of 1990 football hooliganism was suddenly being viewed as a growing serious problem. In early November a fan was shot dead when Sachsen Leipzig played FC (formerly the hated Dynamo) Berlin, and a symbolic unofficial match between West and East Germany, scheduled for the twenty-first of that month in Leipzig to mark the creation of a single national football federation, was cancelled amid fears of violence. Before the 1990–91 season was over, the hooligan fans of FC Berlin – by now, bizarrely, attracting amid their sparse following neo-Nazis – would perpetrate an orchestrated riot in Rostock, smashing seventeen shop fronts and fighting the police, before destroying their homeward train. An editorial in *Kicker* magazine, in words quite prophetic, had opined that thugs were "using the game as a platform for their excesses and aspirations, whatever these may be".

Measures were taken, particularly among the bigger clubs of western Germany who were anxious to protect their public image. One of these initiatives was the 'Fan Projekt' whereby supporters' groups and club officials held regular forums to foster a sense of positive involvement and goodwill. Eastern Germany would retain its different kettle of piranhas, though. And the problems within the former GDR, ultimately, would be hugely instrumental in Chancellor Kohl's being driven from power and in Germany's national football team becoming a vehicle for far-right extremists to make their point. Their insensitivity when following that team to Brussels in August 1995 for a match to celebrate the opening of the King Baudouin Stadium, the rebuilt Heysel, when 117 were arrested, was a mere indicator of what would follow.

The heady mixture of an unleashed freedom of expression and a sense of reclaimed nationalism was a natural factor in the boisterousness of the newly unbounded east. When the unrelenting reality of economic hardship set in and its abandoning hopelessness proved Helmut's assurances to be false, boisterousness would turn to savagery and pointed protest. Burgeoning neo-Nazism in the east, graphically illustrated by television footage of arson attacks on the hostels of *gastarbeiter* and asylum-seekers deemed to be an intrusive drain upon already meagre resources, gave fuel to those similarly minded activists elsewhere. These became disaffected all the more by the prospect of their national sovereignty's being diluted – and the symbolic mark's being killed off – by some Euro-State. For the latter, it seemed the French had much to answer ...

It was an upsurge not unnoticed by a millionaire publisher in Munich called Gerhard Frey, who was quick to see the value of distributing his propagandist leaflets at football matches. Bankrolling the German People's Union (DVU), a virtually structureless but emphatically racist neo-Nazi party, Frey entered the political conflict on an anti-foreigner, anti-euro, Germany-for-the-Germans ticket. His agenda was one of fomenting unrest to derail Kohl's integrating-Europe train, his nationalistic stance one that engaged the forsaken jobless and the callous chauvinists.

In the spring of 1998, Saxony-Anhalt bore the highest unemployment rate in Germany, 23.4%, and the slowest growth rate. In its state election of April 26th an anti-Kohl vote, whilst the Social Democrats of Gerhard Schröder held sway, saw the DVU achieve a wholly unprecedented and quite dramatic thirteen per cent in the ballot box, the heaviest showing for an extreme-right party in Germany since World War Two. With unemployment in eastern Germany as a whole standing at over seventeen per cent (and with four million jobless throughout the country) five months later, and with the various right-wing parties eschewing rivalry to form a concerted protest platform, Helmut Kohl, western Europe's longest serving leader, was thrown out of office after sixteen years in the September general election. Schröder, a leftist, became the new

Chancellor, but at least was viewed in the east as a pragmatist committed to reducing unemployment, even if his coalition government was drawn to European union and even the introduction of dual citizenship for many foreign residents.

Three months before that general election, dark forces had been at work in France.

Daniel Nivel, a 43-year-old senior sergeant and married with two sons, had seen service in Corsica. Now, he belonged to a mobile police unit stationed in Arras and was allocated service in Lens. A man living in the tiny village of Tollent, where Nivel was born, would say, "You might expect danger in Corsica. But Lens?" With a population of only 30,000, Lens was a synonym in France for stoicism, its battlefield history never more pronounced than in World War One when the carnage of the Western Front practically razed it, and its hardships underlined by the decline of its coal industry. But its townsfolk were looked upon as salt-of-the-earth, and its football fans – most of the townsfolk – who'd appropriately just celebrated their first-ever French Championship were considered the country's best. Thus Lens, among the most eager and most honoured, became the least populated town ever to stage the World Cup Finals. Into this mood, on the third weekend of June 1998, came people with a different sort of party in mind.

The planners were predominantly from Hamburg, which had developed its own nest of right-wing extremists. The police chief of Pas de Calais, Daniel Cadoux, noted that these were "well-organised, ruthlessly efficient and sober". It transpired that they'd even used websites to co-ordinate their assault. The plan was to lay into the police, uniformed symbols of a historic enemy to which post-World War II German politicians had behaved delicately, even as Der Vaterland made sacrifices towards a French-inspired Euroblob, and into any swarthy-looking foreigners, be they north African or Yugoslav. 300,000 of the latter, the Balkan conflict having raged, had swelled Germany's immigrant problem. From Brunswick and, particularly, Hanover, came more blood-brothers, resentful and cold, spoiling for a fight. One flag. Theirs.

Germany's drawn match against Yugoslavia on Sunday 21st June was their second in group F. It was Nivel's last. On a coach from Hanover was 27-year-old Marcus Warnecke, co-owner of a tattoo and body-piercing shop and a member of the NSDA, National Socialist German Workers. Whether he and his cohorts found any Serbs to assault is unclear – in general terms, I personally wouldn't have fancied their chances, since Belgrade is the only place abroad I've felt distinctly ill-at-ease in following Albion. (During our 1979

UEFA Cup quarter-final there against Red Star, two of the 95,000 crowd, which included an organised ruck of troublesome Partizan fans, got killed no less in the fiercest of brawling, a fact unreported in the English media.) For that matter, nor were there any reported incidents after Germany got stuffed by Croatia in Lyon. The notion that Germans are bullies has more than a bit of credence.

Around twenty Germans, Warnecke prominent, trapped the lone Daniel Nivel, brought him to his knees with a wooden streetsign, bludgeoned him countless times about the head with his own teargas launcher, then stuck the boot in for good measure. When they ran away, he remained a toppled refuse sack leaking red pus into the gutter.

It was estimated that over six hundred 'category C' hooligans – the worst kind – had entered France from Germany that weekend. Two-thirds were estimated to be neo-Nazis. Among the 96 arrested were Warnecke and Karl-Heinz Elschner, both charged with attempted murder. Within a month, in Hanover, three more would face the same charge. Thankfully, Nivel would eventually emerge from his six-week coma; but remain brain-damaged. The French Interior Ministry had meanwhile revealed that one thousand had been arrested on various charges over the tournament. Its head, Jean-Pierre Chevènement, thought English hooliganism had been "pretty dispersed" but the German brand "much more organised and methodical".

In my experience of following England abroad – and Luxembourg has twice been subjected to our own excesses, a particularly infamous rampage having taken place back in October 1977 – I have seen all too sizeable minorities of boors and people, if not actually bent on causing trouble, then only too ready to react to those who come out to confront and provoke them (but who have often, like most of us, been easily ill-judged by a dishonourable press when either culpability has lain elsewhere or desired headlines have required a pronounced degree of manipulation).

The attack on Daniel Nivel was something else. He was the victim of a dispassionate, malign brutality beneath any beery, blimpish Englishman.

Chapter 13

Chinese Whispers

Hong Kong: South China v Golden 10/3/98

As the light faded, the shabby old woman cast off from the jetty with her supper wrapped in polythene. I watched her paddle ever so slowly across Sok Kwu Wan's small harbour atop what looked for all the world like a mattress, and marvelled at her agility, for she must have been eighty at least. Home itself sat on the water, a tented raft amid the fish farms of rural Lamma Island.

Around the same time, a burglary was taking place on the teeming, towering north side of Hong Kong Island at the apartment of a finance company's executive director, netting uninsured cash, a Rolex watch, diamond earrings and other jewellery to a total value of £5,400.

Thus was the disparity of Hong Kong, our erstwhile outpost whose dubious acquisition Lord Palmerston had derided as "barren, with hardly a house upon

Chinese dwellings, Lamma Island

it", underscored. A place where Western high-flyers can carry their suits from money-chasing Central by day into the flashing flesh-pits of Wan Chai by night and help Triad-run Filipino girls send back a crust to parent hovels across the South China Sea. A place, too, where British footballers in the twilight of their career have earned a last, large loaf.

On the historic day of 1st July 1997 two disparate worlds were rejoined politically, albeit on a very peculiar basis; and with somewhat profounder curiosity than that provoked by Joy's hirsute abdomen gyrating atop Club Lipstick's bar, we watch for the effect upon this no-longer crown colony of a retrieving fatherland where democracy and human rights have no harbour. A quaint football scene will have to paddle carefully as well.

A girlie bar in Kowloon called Bottoms Up might consider itself Hong Kong's most famous drinking hole on account of the fact it featured briefly in a 1974 James Bond film, but it's never been recreated behind a byeline at Wembley as Scotland's goalkeeper fetched the ball out of his net. That accolade belongs to Causeway Bay's The Jump, a very pricey favourite of expats which was famously paid a visit by England's finest at the close of their Far East trip just prior to Euro '96, and where Paul Gascoigne in particular fell prey to those who would use a camera as a toilet brush. This was the night, never mind with permission and without breaking curfew, that to have birthday booze poured down your throat became a treasonable crime. But on the afternoon that Gazza pointedly re-enacted The Jump's 'dentist's chair' in celebration of his magnificent goal against the Jocks, it would be sanctimony that choked.

Three-quarters of a mile westward along Lockhart Road, scene of much off-duty partying during the Vietnam War, into Wan Chai, rather more upmarket today than when it formed Suzie Wong's world, and Dean might have spluttered a little now in our hotel. His window installation company had a contract to help build Hong Kong's new airport, and before each of his numerous visits he'd ask if anyone else fancied coming along for the ride. In March 1998 not one took up his offer. Five of us did; and somehow his contract survived, on an average of three hours' kip.

Not that the trip – sadly, an insufficient week of it – was drinking only. If my introductions had consisted of indeed a fashionable Western bar called Joe Bananas, a wonderful tram notice not to open windows in the event of typhoons, and a view from Victoria Peak that was even more stunning at night – the archetypal postcard panorama that had shaped my simple preconception of Hong Kong – then the touring would indeed be rewarded by sights and sounds of a more enlightening nature. This was far from being just a dense forest of skyscrapers pressing against an ever-busy harbour, some improbable City of London jammed between a totalitarian devil and a deep blue sea.

Lamma, one of more than two hundred islands which together with the Kowloon Peninsula and pastoral New Territories comprise the region's total area of over a thousand square kilometres, was almost tranquillity itself. Stepping from the ferry, and barely encountering a soul along the way, we followed a trail for an hour's hike through its hilly greenery, past a Tin Hau temple and a remote nest of ramshackle dwellings where two Chinese families sat outside playing chequers below washing lines hung from corrugated iron. It was at this point that I really felt that part of the world I'd come to. Five years previously I'd sat alone in a small fountained courtyard at midnight in Colonia, Uruguay, surrounded thickly by unfamiliar foliage and strange sounds, and said to myself: this is South America. Now, this was south-east Asia. Perhaps my imagination overdid it – to get into the mood, I'd stayed up all night watching *The Deer Hunter* before heading off for Heathrow! – but when the others walked far too quickly ahead and I had solitude amid the wilderness, the rattle from a cement plant might just have been ....well. Those tented rafts seemed redolent of something, too. "Michael! There's rats in here!" mimicked part-Irish Bill: so I wasn't the only one picturing wildly. For that matter, as well, a mere four hundred miles away in that vast republic lay the peasant roots of Chairman Mao himself, and Lamma helped engage such thoughts like Lockhart Road never could.

I ended up engaging the police in an attempt to locate Hong Kong's national stadium. Despite its three-tiered 40,000 seats, a recent state-of-the-art construction boasting spectacularly arched roofing, and according to its official pamphlet the "home of sports and entertainment events in the territory" (including the International Rugby Sevens), it failed to show on any handout tourist map. I knew only that it was roughly where Wan Chai meets Happy Valley, and that it nestled against jungly trees some way below the straining concrete skyline. Amazingly, Westerners I asked near the unmissable racecourse – an infinitely more popular theatre of entertainment – knew even less. Thus it was that, inside a police station, an officer kindly drew me directions: on the back of a crime message, which is how I also learned the minute details of that burglary, including the dubious role of the maid.

Having been quickly ejected by a security guard, a more benign stadium official subsequently spent half an hour showing me around. "For football," he told me, "it hosts only big games – national matches, guest tournaments, cup finals." In fact, although he didn't say so, this lovely setting was an embodiment of the Hong Kong FA's fears.

For all that it was the English who codified the game we know today and spread that gospel around the globe, the Chinese can lay claim to having been the first to play a rudimentary version of football, military training during the Han dynasty over two thousand years ago involving 'tsu chu', 'tsu' meaning to kick and 'chu' meaning ball. Yet for all that, modern football's development left the Far East a backwater: understandable when one considers factors such as geography, finance, politics and, indeed, psyche. But when the Asian Football Confederation was formed in 1954, its first four presidents would be gentlemen of Hong Kong whilst another, Lee Wai-Tong, would be its general secretary for an embryonic eleven years. The 1950s, indeed, saw Hong Kong at the forefront of the Asian game. However, although North Korea would castrate Italy and petrify every Portuguese bar Eusébio in 1966, though South Korea would be not merely cannon fodder in subsequent World Cups, and though Japan and China would eventually establish meaningful domestic league structures, Hong Kong's status would diminish into a Far East afterthought, except for ageing mercenaries from abroad. So as South Korea and Japan prepare to co-host the 2002 World Cup Finals – a first for Asia, which indeed provides a quarter of FIFA's membership and two-fifths of the world's population – the role of Hong Kong becomes increasingly peripheral.

In 1998 came talk of China's integrating two Hong Kong clubs: an appalling prospect for the HKFA's Vincent Yuen, anxious that the national stadium should continue to be a stage for World Cup qualifiers not Chinese league matches. That latter scenario indeed spelt an erosion of identity that could lead to loss of FIFA membership. "They know," said Yuen, "that we are working very hard despite our problems, and that we want to stay on the international agenda. But if we were to become one unit ...."

Beijing's tentacles aside, consider also the following: despite its population of six and a half million – double that of Uruguay, twice World Champions – Hong Kong has less than 150 football pitches (one I saw on Hennessy Road in Wan Chai was tarmac shared with basketball, where the ball used was peculiarly half regulation size); spectators, for whom satellite TV readily offers comparison of the local standard with European leagues, are voting with their feet (some may welcome the sight of better-tuned Chinese outfits); many of those mercenaries themselves have left; the Hong Kong League is a mere pot-pourri of rootless clubs, unstably the visage of businessmen owners. And then there's the national team itself. My visit coincided with the ground-breaking enlistment of a Brazilian coach, Sebastiao Araujo, whose influence would extend to youth football – "the key to our future," said HKFA chairman Victor Hui Chun-fui – and whose demand of rescheduling the league

Hong Kong's national stadium

season to accommodate three days' coaching each week of the national squad would also be met. He had his work cut out; less than a year later, in the Asian Games, Hong Kong would lose 0–6 to Oman and 0–5 to Thailand. As 1999 unfolded, too, in protest at a FIFA decision to award it only four World Cup Finals places including those of the co-hosts, Asia would threaten a tournament boycott. But, in the face of comparative Far East heavyweights and the oil-endowed Arab nations, what chance ever Hong Kong anyway?

That flagship stadium seems only the grand bequest of a strangled pioneer.

Dean led us to another, by way of a short underground ride across to Kowloon. This was the tiny Mongkok Stadium, a rare space amid the concrete jungle that bustled in the dark early evening, a railway line clattering along one side, temporary seats erected at each end, the place virtually coverless and almost scraped by roaring jumbo jets on their evasive approach to old Kai Tak. Bags of chickens' feet were on sale for the peckish, cans of Tsingtao beer carrying the message "Congratulation on Hong Kong's Return to CHINA" for the thirsty. Just 1,683 folk – we six looked the only Westerners among them – paid their fiver, and the football they witnessed could best be summed up by a barman in the nearby Tin Lung Pub on Fa Yuen Street, who beforehand had persistently indulged in a particularly unedifying but shameless Chinese custom, that of gobbing on the spot.

What a strange assembly it was. No colours, no banners (prohibited), no partisanship, no encouragement, no emotion, barely a noise: some nattering interspersed with laughter at the error-strewn fare. The overall impression was one of mere onlookers in an atmosphere of cynical resignation. Such had been the tail-end world of Happy Valley's Tony Morley and Golden's Gus Caesar, whilst the Golden Select XI that entertained England at the national stadium in May 1996 had included the names of Hesford, Duxbury and Fairweather. Lucrative, though: Brits out here were often drawing wages that compared with England's first division, even if their ability did not. In some cases, however, this was less a winding-down than a new lease of life. Ex-Tottenham goalkeeper Peter Guthrie left a Gosforth supermarket to try his luck in Hong Kong and would end up representing it against Chile.

With the territory's possessing a mere handful of stadia, Ericsson League matches are neutrally allocated thereto, and tonight's pairing at Mongkok put South China against Golden, the former a rarity in that it was actually the long-standing team of a sports organisation (South China Athletic Association). The latter, typically, was a publicity tool of an electronics company, though it had recently hit financial problems and familiar faces had left. The frequent lack of elementary ball control, the passes born merely of hope which were all too often miscued anyway, the paucity of vision, were redolent of Sunday mornings – which explains how young Brit nonentities, too, though below-grade at home, could carve out a comfortable living here, especially with their greater physical presence. As for tactical nous, that was personified by Golden's midget Chinese sweeper, of whom I had a good view at our end in the first half.

Ludicrously, like some short-trousered goalhanger at the wrong end of the playground, he forever patrolled no further than twenty yards forward of his goalline – and witless South China didn't capitalise. Without a shred of doubt, of all games involving professional footballers, this was the worst standard I'd ever seen. No Nakatas here; nor even a Fan Zhiyi.

Taking part, however, were two noteworthy characters, one who'd achieved significance already in this part of the world but the other soon to be branded with shame. Having had their early lead pegged back with ten minutes left, South China's injury-time match-winner was interval substitute Dale Tempest, whose ten successful years in Hong Kong had seen him not only top the goalscoring charts but also become a television personality through his roles of commentator and presenter. Tempest was about to return to England, and would then offer a trenchant view of his erstwhile habitat: "It's ridiculous that while clubs spend lots of money on foreign players, the coaches are all locals, usually just a friend of the owner; and there isn't one good coach in the whole of the league." A team-mate of Tempest tonight was nevertheless considered one of the brightest goalkeeping prospects in the Far East. Sixteen months later he might have found himself in a huge spotlight when South China hosted European Champions Manchester United in a full-house national stadium with television coverage beamed around the world. Instead, Kevin Lok Kar-win languished in jail, banned from football for life, one of four players found guilty of fixing a World Cup qualifier against Thailand in 1997, just one in a long list of scandals involving bribery and illegal gambling that the wager-mad Far East has thrown up. Maybe Hong Kong, where horse racing provides the only legal form of sports gambling, could try following Singapore, whose league in early 1999 became the first in Asia to authorise domestic football betting in a bid to combat corruption and raise funds too.

Maybe that's some way down the list of the people's concerns, though.

The weather was unkind during the official ceremony, the sight of Chris Patten not only morose but rain-sodden too as the Union Jack came down doubtless providing added satisfaction for Beijing. Such was the handback of that territory which the British had grabbed largely through the havoc of unleashing opium onto China during trade disputes around the turn of the nineteenth century, and whose sovereignty had forever stuck in Beijing's throat. Now a 'Special Administrative Region of China', Hong Kong is nevertheless allowed in theory to maintain for fifty years more those social, economic and legal systems it enjoyed under Britain: "one country, two systems" as Beijing put it.

In truth, so far, the arrangement has largely been honoured, perhaps best exemplified by the fact that although Chinese security forces detained human rights activists and closed off Tiananmen Square on the tenth anniversary of its massacre, Hong Kong residents were again allowed to mark the occasion in memory of those who, demonstrating pro-democracy and against corruption, had been ruthlessly gunned down.

Fifty years. Common sense surely dictates, though, that Beijing will want to meanwhile realign the present differences to ensure that only one system is eventually arrived at smoothly. Already, real legislative power in Hong Kong rests pointedly in the hands of Beijing's appointees, democratic ethics absent. Whilst the prevailing system in China nowadays allows a market economy (and Hong Kong's new government would deal very cutely indeed with the Asian economic crisis of the late nineties), the one-party communist state has been rigorously enforced, even to the point of its clamping down in mid-1999 upon some bizarre mystic cult, Falun Gong, perceived to be a mobilising threat. So it would seem that the real disquiet in Hong Kong lies not in any denial of its following a capitalist mentality but in its now being governed indeed by people to whom transparency has been foreign and dictatorship the norm.

Who knows? In an ever-changing world, China might come to realise that international acceptance is desirable, and towards that end might help redress its criminal abuse of Tibetans by granting them umbrella autonomy, might bridge its gap with rebel Taiwan, might renounce its development of neutron bombs, and might produce avian pigs. Whatever else, though, Hong Kong is now China's. They say nothing's certain in football, but one thing surely is: fifty years or less, the Hong Kong Football Association's days as a national body are numbered.

It seems typical, today, that whilst my beloved, underachieving Albion should effectively have done China a favour all those years ago by accepting its 1978 invitation to famously tour there, a mere tool of its diplomatic overtures, twenty-odd years later overachieving Manchester United should practically invade to milk it – and the rest of the Far East – like some footballing McDonald's, capitalising upon massive "support" there by opening theme parks, Red Cafés with video screens, superstores selling its branded merchandise, replica shirts to the fore (counterfeiting of the latter may pose Old Trafford a problem, however). Rupert Murdoch's bid for United had Asia hugely in mind, too.

So this is football in 2000. Businessmen chasing millions of pounds from people who will never see that team in the flesh, as if football and flesh needn't necessarily fuse any more. I almost wonder nevertheless if United might eventually dare the ultimate, and how symbolic that would be too. On my first afternoon in Hong Kong, perhaps appropriately in Joe Bananas, I got talking to a Dutchman called Hans who'd arrived twenty years earlier as a tennis coach. Now, he made his living by selling female sex aids.

Bibliography and Acknowledgements

The following books were especially helpful:

"World Soccer from A to Z" – Norman Barrett (ed) (Pan Books, 1973)

"The Footballer's Companion" – Brian Glanville (ed) (Eyre & Spottiswoode, 1962)

"Sport Behind The Iron Curtain" – Simon Freeman and Roger Boyes (Proteus, 1980)

"My Name Is Eusébio" – Eusébio da Silva Ferreira (Routledge & Kegan Paul, 1967)

"The Best Game In The World" – Terry Venables (Century, 1996)

"The Sunday Times History Of The World Cup" – Brian Glanville (Times Newspapers Ltd, 1973)

"Association Football" (Vols 3 & 4) – A.H. Fabian and Geoffrey Green (eds) (Caxton, 1960)

"The Football Grounds Of Europe" – Simon Inglis (Collins Willow, 1990)

The following publications were also particular sources of information:

"World Soccer"

"The Times"

Thanks also to:

Lonely Planet Publications, Bill Ahern, Steve Munday, Mick Hamblett and Simon Wright for their assistance.

And I hope "Jimmy" survived to be happy in the new Germany.

Also of interest:

BLEAK & BLUE: 22 years at the Manchester Academy of Football Farce

Craig Winstanley

A great read for all Blues fans and for football fans everywhere, Bleak and Blue is a hugely entertaining record of the joys and misery of two decades of the history of Manchester City Football Club. A big book in every way, the author's fanzine-style writing covers all major games in minute detail, relentlessly pursuing a club which could again be a great football club. "An essential book for all Blues fans; and for all football fans....It's a brilliant read, even if you know nothing - and don't care - about football " SOUTH MANCHESTER REPORTER. £8.95

WHEN FRIDAY NIGHT WAS COUNTY NIGHT: Stockport footballing memories

Barry Cheetham

A fan's personal history of Stockport County FC between 1952 and 1998, this tells of the frustration, heartache and occasional joy in supporting your local club. Essential reading for supporters of the Hatters but sure to appeal to all football fans – it is spiked with the gallows humour and ready wit of the terraces. The book also provides an excellent social history of what it was like to grow up in the fifties and sixties, as it follows seven supporters who meet as teenagers and establish a lifelong friendship cemented by their love of football. £7.95

All of our books are available through booksellers. In case of difficulty, or for a free catalogue, please contact:

SIGMA LEISURE, 1 SOUTH OAK LANE, WILMSLOW, CHESHIRE SK9 6AR.
Phone: 01625-531035
Fax: 01625-536800.
E-mail: info@sigmapress.co.uk
Web site: http//www.sigmapress.co.uk
MASTERCARD and VISA orders welcome.